No
Bottom

XOXOX
PRESS

Gambier, Ohio

**for more information
visit:
www.nobottomauthor.com**

No
Bottom

In Conversation
with Barry Lopez

Mike Newell (signature)

Mike
Newell

XOXOX
PRESS

Gambier, Ohio

Photographs by Phyllis & Mike Newell
Cover image © 2007 JupiterImages Corporation
Cover design by Jerry Kelly and Tarah Gaa
Production editing by Helen Stayman
Book design by Jerry Kelly

ISBN 978-1-880977-07-1

Published by XOXOX Press
102 Gaskin Ave., Box 51
Gambier, OH 43022
xoxoxpress.com

Distributed in the U.S. by Small Press Distribution
Berkeley, CA—spdbooks.org

Printed in USA
Printing Arts Press, Mount Vernon, OH
First softcover edition—April 2008

Library of Congress Cataloging-in-Publication Data

Newell, Mike.
    No bottom : in conversation with Barry Lopez / by Mike Newell. — 1st ed.
    p. cm.
    ISBN 978-1-880977-07-1
    1. Lopez, Barry Holstun, 1945—Criticism and interpretation. 2. Lopez, Barry
Holstun, 1945—Interviews. 3. Authors, American—20th century—Interviews. I.
Title.
    PS3562.O67Z77 2008
    813'.54—dc22

                                    2007046614

Contents

for Arnold G. Tucker and Patrick Meanor
~ *journey helpers*

Prologue

Not only from the mouth of Bracken Cave at twilight
where ravenous free-tailed mammals in true flight issue
from a subterranean sphere, how their peregrinations
bewray Bacchic appetites.
Reluctantly, too, from the aura of an inflammatory literature
and from the footnotes of county cooperative bulletins
which besiege the ear with gurglings
of those hairy-legged brethren.
Occasionally not unlike the torment upon waking to the
    flutterings of wayward young.
More often akin to nectar-gatherers that absently pollinate
and to the little browns that wallow amongst mooncakes
    in star-weary skies.
Self-absorbed in nocturnal gluttony
their Immelmann-turns rend oodles of winged revelers.
Translucent droppings of chitin affirm
the unfathomable bounty of an earthly sojourn.

MN
Hartwick, NY
January 2007

"The way we take care of ourselves
is by taking care of each other."
Barry Lopez

Foreword

I stumbled across *Arctic Dreams* in the mid-'80s. I would like to believe the seeds of that rendezvous were sown years earlier, when I crisscrossed the tundra and mountain ranges of Alaska as a wildland firefighter. Whether that fateful encounter owed to the mythological intrigue I still associated with a fabled landscape remains elusive. What I am grateful for is the act of having hauled that enchanting book off its shelf and slowly thumbed its pages.

Barry Lopez's nonfiction bestseller and National Book Award winner initiated me to the gravitational pull of an extraordinary imagination. I intuited an orbiting of ideas whose cohesive sublimity triggered a tectonic-plate shift in my thinking. At the time I did not know the range of his writing talents. I soon devoured his earlier works in fiction and nonfiction. His writing leavened word choice and delivery. The more I read the more I marveled at his storytelling gifts. He seamlessly morphed genres. I came to appreciate how he could rub a poet's yearning for the accuracy and the aptness of words—especially the echoes of their exquisite, internal pulses—against the philosopher's stone.

The stirrings for *No Bottom* originated in 1999. I had been contracted to write an article on Barry's short stories for a popular lit-bio series. My letter of introduction to his agent, Jim Rutman at Sterling Lord Literistic, generated a telephone call from Barry. He immediately put me at ease by asking *my* permission for us to address each other on a first-name basis. He agreed to an interview and even suggested lodging overlooking the McKenzie River. My wife, Phyllis, and I flew from Upstate New York to Oregon in late October. Over the course of a few days, Barry, Phyllis and I yammered incessantly. Even our taped conversations were unrehearsed and informal. Our vagaries of topic dead ended, side barred and segued. Sometimes we sat on the cabin's back deck with the timpanic boomings of the McKenzie suggesting counterpoints to our cartwheeling dialogues. At other times, Barry drove us to a setting for a scene from *River Notes* or across a plank bridge and into the mountain range of the Three Sisters. It was in this landscape that Barry introduced us to the Pacific madrone, an evergreen whose unique features include a peeling, reddish bark and flowers that yield honey. In all venues, Barry was generous, genuine and genial. He entrusted us with rare documents and, at one point, with a copy of "Emory Bear Hands' Birds" in its final-draft throes; with personal stories whose tones would educe rollicking guffaws or heartwrenching reflection; and with insights into a personality imbued with humility.

What then followed, for me, was a two-year immersion to ferret out all minutiae pertaining to Barry's life story, literary development and professional achievements. I haunted local college libraries for samplers of his early writings and located—amid poetry, book reviews, a movie review, how-to articles and a penchant for photography—a short story published in college that contained the genesis for one of his major themes. I trolled the Internet for interviews and marveled at their spiritual essence. I then sought first editions, so I could measure the designs of their dust jackets against the accompanying short stories. I beseeched magazine staff for difficult-to-locate or out-of-print articles, as I sought his grounding in social consciousness. What has unfurled is, to me, unprecedented and has no bottom.

Barry's writings strike a chord with diverse cultures of all ages and inspire creative responses. From his short stories alone, fine-book presses publish collectable, limited editions; artists and musicians collaborate; playwrights adapt; and science professors make abstract concepts obvious. *Of Wolves and Men* approaches allegorical implications in its uncanny plea for tolerance. The odyssey and the quest for personal growth in *Crow and Weasel* appeal to the child; to the academic student at every stage; to the betrothed; and, not surprisingly, to the terminally ill. Barry's boundless intellect and capacity to unmask an event, to reveal its genome so to speak, manifests in how he champions the marginalized in *A Rediscovery of North America* and in recognizing the physical "dark" of nighttime as a natural resource.

Throughout my queries and writing of the lit-bio article, I corresponded with Barry so as to inculcate clarity and accuracy of factual material. However, readers should not assume that he endorses any particular critical discussion or interpretation, including mine. That would be anathema to the nature of a writer who makes room for every reader's active participation. I strove to have the article's factual integrity worthy of a scholar's reference, without the usual drone of objective dryness, and, yet, be accessible to the curious. In my zeal, I strayed from the formulaic restrictions of the lit-bio series. There were simply more compelling dimensions to the author and his work than the senior editor preferred. Due to creative differences, I withdrew my manuscript for consideration.

For a time, I was content to tweak the lit-bio manuscript; to quietly track Barry's work; to incorporate his writings into my teachings in a program for at-risk teenagers as well as in a college introductory writing course; and to roister with likeminded aficionados. I quickly abandoned any pretense of attempting a scholarly baedeker. The rich, on-going array of Barry's work, of creative responses, of critical commentaries and of awards simply outpaces scholarly impulses. For an overview, readers should visit his website, www.barrylopez.com, which is an excellent source of information and is faithfully updated.

To preserve my existing research at the time, I accepted Barry's invitation to send a copy of the unpublished lit-bio manuscript to William Tydeman at Texas Tech University, where Barry's archives are held in the Southwest/Special Collections

Library. In consideration for the depth of insider knowledge that Barry had graciously provided me, I also gave a copy of the manuscript to Dr. Daniel Payne, at the State University College at Oneonta, New York. Dr. Payne subsequently wrote a compelling and insightful article on Barry's short story books for the *Dictionary of Literary Biography* series. Interestingly, the editor of a prominent literary journal offered to publish the taped conversations. (Without disclosing their contents, I had enthusiastically alerted a mutual friend to the tapes' existence.) I declined. Barry and I had yet to navigate through them. I did long to find avenues for a wider audience, but coalescing the manuscript, tapes and correspondence remained elusive for another three years.

Meanwhile, in the spring of 2001, Phyllis and I enjoyed a presentation by Barry at the Rosamond Gifford Lecture Series in Syracuse, NY. The following year I was honored when Barry asked me, along with others, to recommend selections of his short stories for *Vintage Lopez*. Random House was launching a series through its Vintage imprint to connect readers with the works of modern, influential writers. In his unassuming way, Barry wrote me, "I find my name in this list...." I was delighted to play a background role in bringing Barry to SUNY Oneonta, in October 2002, for the Mills Lecture Series. Last fall, Phyllis and I traveled to the Northshire Bookstore in Manchester, Vermont to hear Barry's presentation of *Home Ground: Language for an American Landscape*.

I continued to listen to the October tapes. Initially, they had served to flesh out my memory for the lit-bio article. Later, I would listen so as to revisit our conversations and to freefall among their innuendoes, as I visualized Barry pausing to take an internal inventory or to gaze and comment upon kayakers in the river below. In those re-listenings, I came to appreciate the tapes' uniqueness and tantalizing distinctions.

Even with the remorseless, hydraulic grind of the McKenzie in the background and amid the artless cacophonies of conversation, they resonate. The tapes are unfettered, although amorphous. They radiate sincerity, passion and often self-effacement. What is also compelling are the laniappes that provide glimpses into the thought-processes of an intensely private and remarkable individual. This realization prompted the boof for *No Bottom*. I wrote to Barry about my publication plans. Despite an incessant clamoring for his time and creative energy, he recently edited the following interview so as to provide one that is unique, has no overlaps to earlier published interviews and is singular in theme.

   No Bottom is a snapshot. Its core energy flows, as ghost light, from artifacts garnered between 1999 and 2002. Accompanying the interview is a critical discussion of Barry's short story books: *Desert Notes, River Notes, Winter Count, Field Notes, Light Action in the Caribbean* and *Resistance*. Initially, I hesitated to reach for newer material, including the eclectic stories in *Resistance,* published in 2004 and chosen for the H.L. Davis Award for Short Fiction in 2005. To omit this notable body of stories seemed contrary. Its stylistic and thematic connections to earlier works were too compelling for me to overlook. The Boswellian footprint of *No Bottom* humbly strives to bear witness to a gifted, remarkable human being. Barry Lopez's life and letters salve the wounds of timeless angst.

MN
Hartwick, NY
October 2007

Conversations with Barry Lopez
October 22-23, 1999

Newell: I'm intrigued by what you suggest in your work about social animals adapting, changing over time. For example, that wolves—being social animals—might change over time as a species. Is that a thought Western biologists generally subscribe to?

Lopez: I don't know. That was originally the insight of a Nunamiut man named Justus Mekiana, reported to me by Bob Stephenson, and made many years ago at Anaktuvuk Pass in the Brooks Range [Alaska]. Justus looked up from his spotting scope—he was watching a wolf doing something he'd never seen before—he looked up and wondered aloud whether wolves might still be evolving, in the way that people had moved from bands of hunter-gatherers into more complicated systems of social organization, like those that evolved in Ur in lower Mesopotamia or in pre-contact Central and South America. We're now, obviously, even more complex as a species, organized around technologies like the car and the world wide web and around political philosophies like "globalization." The suggestion by Mekiana is, to me, something to be attentive to. I don't believe any one civilization has all the answers to life's questions. I don't believe in "progress" in the sense of making improvements so much as I believe in evolution, in change through time. We seem to have numerous, intractable social problems—child abuse, greed, infidelity, institutionalized injustice, corrupt behavior in public office. To one degree or another this was part of the Roman Empire and of Greece in Alexander's time. It emerged with the revolutions that Bolivar set in motion in South America and with the African independence movements of the '60s. Everywhere you go you find this.

Newell: Around the planet, it doesn't matter where you are?

Lopez: Yes. Saying so-called underdeveloped or fourth-world or "primitive" societies are "backward" by definition is a kind of whistling in the dark. In my experience, traditional people have managed to live successfully with most of these intractable social ills, and occasionally to be even better at it than we are.

The reason for someone like me to go out and try to learn something about wolves—which means speaking with or apprenticing myself to traditional people—is to be able to structure a story that, by analogy, helps us understand some of the patterns of human life. I never took a course in biology, and I have no professional background with animals to work from. What I learned in college was how to learn, how to teach myself. When I first became acquainted with wolves, I imagined their world as a complex landscape I could enter in some limited way, and in which I could explore questions I found interesting. Someone once told me that *Of Wolves and Men* was a book about tolerance. I don't know what the book is about in a word, but that's close.

I have long had an interest in the nature of intolerance, of prejudice. We continue to suffer as a culture because we haven't created an environment in which disenfranchised people can speak easily. It's two different things, to create a forum and say anybody is welcome, and then to make everyone feel welcome. People who are inarticulate, poorly educated, not white or not Christian don't always feel they're going to be heard. They are often intimidated, to such a degree that they remain silent. Insofar as they do, we suffer as a culture.

Newell: And worse. Look at the tragedies around America, the violent tragedies that occur when people don't feel that they can express themselves.

Lopez: Yes.

Newell: When you write, do you have a desire to know something you didn't know before you began?

Lopez: Well, that's always a part of writing, the discovery on the page, especially in fiction. Nonfiction, for me, is more intentional. You know what you're up to, or you think you do. You want to make some sort of argument, present a point of view the reader understands is yours but which doesn't exclude them, that allows them to participate. In fiction, at least for me, it's more likely that something will happen that I don't anticipate. A character will do something and I'll wonder, "Oh, what's this about?"

I have a strong desire as a writer to know, to ferret out and understand, to demonstrate, which is one reason why my fiction tends to be informed by fact. We're culturally enamored of facts, and we trust factual detail more than we should. Some of my stories achieve what they're after by developing a landscape of facts so convincing it gains the authority of nonfiction. The point I guess is that factual assertions are woven into the Zeitgeist of our time. And I should add that the appearance of fact in my fiction can work to convey a sense of the *narrator's* authority.

As far as I know, nothing in "Ruben Mendoza Vega..." [in *Light Action in the Caribbean*], for example, is actually true. It's merely factual. The entire bibliography at the end of that story—all those book titles—

they're made up. Each book, depending on its politics, has been published in a city in France or Spain or Poland that has a reputation for publishing right-wing literature. The academic journals cited sound plausible, but it's page after page of fabrication. When you read it, it has the rhythms of speech, the pacing, the vocabulary we use when we're offering formal support for our arguments. But when that story began, I really had no idea exactly how Señor Vega was going to try to engage us.

Newell: You've been described as a writer whose fiction falls precisely in that pinstripe area where fact and fiction overlap. For example, in "Remembering Orchards"—

Lopez: The impulse for that story actually—I'm sorry, I interrupted.

Newell: Go ahead.

Lopez: "Remembering Orchards" [in *Light Action in the Caribbean*] grew out of recalling the kind of photographic work I was doing in 1981, when I quit. The thing I most wanted to do then was photograph orchards. One day in my room, years afterward, I sat down at the typewriter with that impulse and this is the story that came out. Though the narrator, I should say, is not me.

Russell Banks advised me once that people miss part of what is going on in my stories. He said, "You use non-autobiographical, 19th-century, first-person narrators, but today the first-person sends signals about autobiography, that the story is about you." My stories are not really about me. They're not disguises I'm trying out. I am no more the character Ruben Mendoza Vega than I am the man narrating "Remembering Orchards." They're people with their own frames of mind. To write them, I enter them.

Newell: A lot of people, I think, missed what was going on in
your earlier work.

Lopez: I wrote *River Notes* when I was twenty-eight. *Desert
Notes* probably when I was twenty-four. *Desert Notes*
is an unselfconscious book. Its forms—for example,
the story called "Introduction"—are a young man's
inventions. *River Notes* is a thicker piece of work, it's
consciously heavier. It's influenced by all this moss
and water here around us, by impenetrable woods,
darkness. A student at a reading at Carleton College
in Minnesota, many years ago, said, "My guess is this
book was generated by some personal tragedy, perhaps the loss of a parent." I remember being shaken,
feeling so exposed, but he was right. It was written in
the wake of my mother's death. *Desert Notes* is playful, but there's no playfulness in *River Notes*. It has a
great sadness running through it, a species of grief.

Jim Andrews, who published *Desert Notes* and
River Notes, understood the different textures of each
book. He had published some of my first stories in
Ave Maria magazine in 1966, and then went on to
found Universal Press Syndicate, with a man named
John McMeel. We stayed in touch, and in 1974 I
showed him *Giving Birth to Thunder*, which was my
transition out of the University of Oregon, where I'd
gone to get an MFA. After the first semester there I
decided I'd do better on my own and I left. Jim
loved the irreverence of *Giving Birth to Thunder*, the
risqué humor. He asked if I'd written anything else.
Well, yes, I said, I'd written a collection of stories
called *Desert Notes*, but I didn't imagine anybody
would be interested in it. I didn't think it would
have any kind of commercial appeal. He said to send
it to him anyway, so I did. He called me the day he

got the manuscript and said not only did he want to
publish *Desert Notes* but he thought it should be my
first book. "This is the way you should be introduced as a writer," he said, "not with *Giving Birth to
Thunder*," which was the first book I'd written. I said
okay, and a few months later I came to Kansas City
and signed a contract with him for a trilogy: *Desert
Notes*, which was finished; *River Notes*, which I was
working on; and a book I didn't know the title of. In
the contract we called it *Animal Notes*. That was
1974. I was twenty-nine.

Newell: Did *Animal Notes* become *Winter Count*?

Lopez: No, *Animal Notes* became *Of Wolves and Men*. The
impulse to write a book about animals was there,
and *Animal Notes* was sort of a space holder for it.
I'd started work on *Of Wolves and Men* early in
1974, but I didn't have a title for it, the vision of
what it would be wasn't clear. The impulse to write
the third book in that trilogy then turned into the
full-blown desire to write *Of Wolves and Men*. When
it did, I told Jim, "I have no idea what the third
book in this trilogy is about, but it's not going to be
called *Animal Notes*, and I don't know when it's
going to come along." I knew I was going to take a
different direction as a writer for a while, knew I
was going to commit more fully to a certain kind of
nonfiction, but I also knew I wanted to break out of
that *Desert Notes* form. And I must have asked
myself sometime in the early 1980s, "How am I
going to get back to the form I followed in *Desert
Notes* and *River Notes*, now that *Winter Count* is finished?" I felt *Winter Count* was an indicator of
where I wanted to go as a fiction writer, but I also
wanted, somehow, to finish the trilogy, to be true to

that intent. Then the work I was doing on *Arctic Dreams* just took over and, for a long period of time, I was in a very nonfictive frame of mind. That's where all of those essays in *Crossing Open Ground* come from, that nonfiction frame of mind.

In the fall of 1979, I went to Ann Arbor, Michigan, to visit Tom Pohrt and his brother Carl, whom I knew better at the time, and their father, Richard Pohrt, one of the most important collectors of Native American material culture in the world. Tom told me he wanted to collaborate on a book, and I said, well, that would be great. I liked Tom's drawing and the sensitivity of the entire Pohrt family to Native American culture and ideas, but didn't know exactly what Tom and I would do. I got a letter from him a few weeks later saying, "Let's not let this go, let's not let this slide away." So, one morning in February of 1980, I sat down in the living room at home—it was just a moment really, when this kind of variegated light was coming through the windows. You know how you feel, the light builds a kind of nest around you, and you feel generative under its influence? I sat down at this small table and wrote out an eight-page narrative that began, "One time two young men, Crow and Weasel, decided to travel farther north than anyone had ever gone."

By that time I had had a lot of exposure to Native American thought, beginning with the work for *Giving Birth to Thunder*, up through traveling with Eskimos in the late seventies and early eighties. I thought I could develop the story organically, out of my own field experience. It took about ten years for Tom to finish the watercolors to his satisfaction. I continued to learn, to apprentice myself to people.

Tom and I had a lot of correspondence back and forth about the book. In 1989, when he was finished, I had to sit down and finally write out the whole story. I'd put myself in something of a box canyon. I knew where the illustrations were going to fall, so I had to write within those boundaries, find a rhythm in sync with the placement of the images across sixty-four pages. I couldn't open up any one part of the story more than another. I was a little bit constrained.

Crow and Weasel was the first big piece of fiction I'd ever attempted—it would end up being about 16,000 words—and the story had been floating around unfinished in my head for ten years. I couldn't really have written it in 1980. In 1985, I traveled to Japan and that began a pattern of international travel which has carried down to the present. This exposure to a lot of different cultures—not just indigenous cultures in North America—gave me what I really needed to be able to write a story about two men who go into a foreign landscape.

Newell: Maybe that's the appeal of it. It became quite a popular book.

Lopez: Well, yes, it went on *The New York Times* fiction list, at about number ten, and I think North Point printed nearly 100,000 copies in those first few months, but I'm trying to paint some kind of picture here, I guess. The impulse to write *Desert Notes* was not an impulse to publish a book. It was an impulse to write out the way I look at things. When I gave Jim Andrews the manuscript for *Desert Notes,* he said, "You told me this story once, about driving your van across an alkali flat, how you got out of it while it was still in gear and walked away, and the van just kept going on without you. You need to put that in here." I said, "Jim, this is a work of fiction. It's not about what *I* did." He said, "No! Write this up. Somehow write this up." And that's where this piece called "Introduction" [in *Desert Notes*] comes from. I had the form of a *Desert Notes* story straight in my head by then, and I shaped what Jim asked for in order to fit the form. I repeated it in *River Notes*, and fifteen years later in *Field Notes*, when I finally finished the trilogy.

So, that early fictive impulse, a particular kind of heightened realism which is rooted in my childhood in California, is developing and I'm growing and changing as a fiction writer, and the early stories mature, and this collection called *Winter Count* comes along. Then I'm buried in *Arctic Dreams*. At the same time, floating in the back of my mind, is this novella-length story *Crow and Weasel*, which comes along in 1990. *Crossing Open Ground* comes out in 1988, a collection of nonfiction from the late seventies through the mid-eighties. It's at that time, late 1989, that I sign a contract with Knopf for a long, complex work of nonfiction, which will require a lot of travel.

Newell: That large book would be...?

Lopez: I don't know yet. It's built around five places I travel to regularly. I'm not sure of all the threads that hold it together. It's a book I don't completely understand yet, because I haven't been through enough. But, you know, looking back from this point, 1999, what I wanted after *Crow and Weasel* was to return to stories like those in *Winter Count,* a book I'm very fond of. I felt I had to finish that trilogy, and *Field Notes* came along as that third book, but its stories, you know, have much more in common with *Winter Count* than they do with the stories in either *Desert Notes* or *River Notes*. This new story collection I've just finished, *The Letters of Heaven*, is the first collection since *Winter Count* that's free of that structure.

Newell: Structure?

Lopez: The imposition of a format from an earlier book. *Winter Count* is arranged around ideas of record keeping. *The Letters of Heaven* is arranged around that clearing between the intellect and the heart. I'm thinking you probably know most of the stories in there, except the new ones.

Newell: Yes, probably I do.

Lopez: If you go from a story like "Thomas Lowdermilk's Generosity" at one end to a story like "Ruben Mendoza Vega..." at the other end, you encounter a wider compass of situations and settings than you do in *Desert Notes* or *River Notes*. Do you know the story called "Benjamin Claire, a North Dakota Tradesman, Writes to the President of the United States?"

Newell: I don't.

Lopez: Or "The Interior of North Dakota?"

Newell: Yes, I've read that.

Lopez: They're both recent stories, but they aren't in the vein or within the scope of *The Letters of Heaven*, so I can't put them in the book.

Newell: You keep saying *The Letters of Heaven*. Did you change the title?

Lopez: No. The title has always been *The Letters of Heaven*. Knopf asked if I would change the title to *Light Action in the Caribbean*. They thought the other title was misleading, that it might signal "religion." I said okay, a decision I'm not really comfortable with. We'll see.

Newell: Could you say something about "The Deaf Girl"? It's an unusually violent story for you.

Lopez: I saw this girl on a hillside in a black frock. An image. Then this man on a porch at night. He was comfortable in his life. He had this air of satisfaction about him, with his cigar, his leisurely travels. He clearly believed he was someone who could inform or help this girl he viewed as a kind of waif. It's not until the last few lines of the story that he realizes things are headed the other way. He understands that she's arrived at a place he's yet to reach. She's not going to go shoot the guy who raped her. That's not what her life is about. She's a terrifying presence to me because she's so fully integrated as a human being she can't be taken out.

Newell: She can't be taken out... you mean inwardly diminished or reduced to a prop?

Lopez: Yeah.

Newell: My word at the end of that story was "reckoning." There's going to be a reckoning over this. She's like one of those Bene Gesseritts out of *Dune*. They've got insights into cosmic machinations that we underlings have no clue about.

Lopez: Yes, that's right.

Newell: That's how I saw the girl. She's way ahead. The story, to adapt your quote from Evan Connell, has no bottom.

Lopez: She gets shot in the head, accidentally, and her father says, "That's it, the hell with L.A. I'm getting my family to a safe place." The father's living in the same world the narrator is living in. He gets his daughter to the safe place, but then a boy comes along. She *knows* she's not safe. She's more aware of what's going on, probably, than anyone in this little town. She has what you might call instructive wounds. The narrator's thinking, "I'm just going to give her the benefit

of my wisdom and control her tendency to violence," but she's way beyond violence. There's no
vengeance in her. A particular kind of scary confrontation, that's her praxis.

Newell: That's why I thought the word reckoning might be
apt.

Lopez: Yeah, reckoning is the right word I think. "Light
Action in the Caribbean," the story that is now the
title story of the collection, is more violent, of course,
than anything I've ever written.

Newell: Are you making a connection with "The Deaf Girl"?

Lopez: If I were aware of any such connections it wouldn't
help my writing. The way I write fiction is to remain
innocent of any point I might be trying to make.

Newell: It's new every time you do it.

Lopez: Yes. You can sit there and say, "You know, I've read a
lot of this author's work and these are the connections
I see." But I don't see them. Somebody has to alert
me to the fact that, say, James Teal in "Teal Creek" [in
Field Notes] bears a resemblance to the hermit in "The
Orrery" [in Winter Count]. Someone could say, "This
writer tends to create this type of character," but I
don't see this insight as a limiting thing, something
that controls me. It's simply how I think about the
world, an approach. If you know, for example, that I
went to Gethsemane as a young man, to Thomas
Merton's monastery in Kentucky, and if you know my
history with monasteries or about my Roman
Catholic education, then of course you could posit
that I might create a character like James Teal. The
interesting thing to me about James Teal, though, is
where did he come from? What in his past generated
his monastic calmness?

Newell: Many of your characters have that monastic calmness.

Many of your stories have purification written into them. You probably know that.

Lopez: No, I mean I don't think of them that way. For me the major difference between a critic's approach and a writer's approach to a story is that the former is analytical about what happens, and so tends to assume the writer has a motive or a plan. I am pursuing no rationale but the character's rationale. If I began thinking of my fiction in terms of monastic characters like James Teal or purification rituals, I could become a kind of caricature of myself. The best thing for me is to have no intention. As soon as you do, I think you're moving into a compromised relationship with the reader. You start wanting the reader to arrive at a predetermined point.

Newell: It occurs to me that some of the techniques I see as patterns in your work maybe you don't care to hear about.

Lopez: No, I don't. I don't want to be aware of my fiction in that way.

Newell: You talk a lot about intolerance and prejudice.

Lopez: Yes.

Newell: It comes out in your stories. But in your latest stories, I see characters engaging in activities and behaviors that didn't occur in the earlier pieces.

Lopez: No, and I'll give you an anecdote that's an illustration of this, an illuminating moment. In 1980 Susan Moldow at Avon Books bought *Desert Notes, River Notes, Giving Birth to Thunder* and *Winter Count* and brought them all out in paperback. We were having lunch in New York. I was telling her about some new stories, and she gave me this look of mock surprise and said, "Oh, so now the characters have names?" Meaning that, early on, I had been reluctant to name

characters, and now, clearly, I'd changed. I have a pro-
tective sense about my private life and I believe most
people feel the same. We live in a society where our
boundaries are penetrated every day by unwanted
people, by unwelcome calls and messages, by aggres-
sive advertising. Virtually none of the characters in
my fiction is based, partly for that reason, on anyone I
know, out of respect for my friends' privacy. Early on,
I wanted to protect even the privacy of my characters. Through anonymity. What's happening in more
recent stories is not an invasion of characters' priva-
cies but a willingness to go in deeper, to reveal more,
to address the darker side of human behavior. The
question for me now is whether I can do that and
not lose something else important, the lyrical celebration of life. I am after more obviously complex lives
in my fiction now.

Newell: There's a divinity in your early writing. Not dignity,
it's beyond dignity.

Lopez: Right, the numinous, I guess. The landscape of the
numinous. A close friend of mine, a wonderful,
insightful man, once said to me, "You'll never write a
novel until you learn to skate," by which he meant
learning to write so that every word didn't have to
count. "You'll never be a novelist until you learn to
skate," he said, "and until you can create characters
and get rid of them." For you, he said, "every character has a quality of life you aren't willing to violate."
I'm interested now in the kind of characters he was
talking about—but I don't have any interest in learning to skate.

Newell: After I read Jim Clavell's *Whirlwind* I was no longer
fretful about the Muslim culture. What he accomplishes, in my mind, parallels some of the work that

you are doing. When you're done writing about something, stereotypes dissolve. Some of your stories quietly address culturally-based anxieties that cause us to unwittingly do harm. The stories themselves become salves to eradicate our xenophobic tendencies. That speaks to divinity. I mention that as a poetic concept... maybe it's a curse, because with that poetic conscience I sense that you can't skate very easily.

Lopez: To me skating is about a more casual relationship with language than the one I want. I told Nick O'Connell in an interview once, in 1985, that my work is my prayer. When you work around language, you have to be aware of your capacity to do harm, by diminishing it, by treating it casually, by being cavalier about the impact a story can have on a human life. If you're going to ask for the reader's vulnerability, it seems to me you have an ethical responsibility to see to it that the reader isn't violated. I know I'm walking on thin ice here, but I'm talking about my own way of looking at this, my conviction that you must be aware of the reader's life, the reader's privacy.

Newell: That's an interesting thought, which isn't often entertained.

Lopez: I see so often now in the movies a tendency to disregard the right of the viewer to be forewarned about violence. To avoid it, you've got physically to get out of the theater.

Newell: That's right.

Lopez: The idea that "controversial" films are always enlightening, that they add a quality of depth to our discourse, is a marketing ploy. A dodge. That's like saying, if you walk down the street and find a man torturing a dog, that standing there and discussing it, deciding whether you're opposed to it or not, is more important than getting the man away from the dog.

Newell: Yeah, I know. I know that feeling. You've said a lot about your fiction, about what you're after there. What about your nonfiction?

Lopez: If you didn't know anything else about my work except what you'd heard of *Arctic Dreams*, or *Of Wolves and Men*, you might assume I was a naturalist, someone writing about nature. I understand that. The natural world, which includes us, is often my setting. My questions, though, even in *Arctic Dreams*, are about tolerance, intimacy, that numinous landscape we spoke of, about justice. I grew up in rural southern California with an intense exposure to the natural world, to light and wind and ocean and desert landscapes. The experience welled up in me in a way that was profoundly emotional. It was fundamental to the shaping of my psyche. At the age of eleven my family moved to New York City, and I became a part of that city in the same way. I went to a private Jesuit school on 83rd Street in Manhattan. I lived on East 35th Street. I went to debutante balls. I went to the theater all the time. I lived an intense, and really joyful, urban life. I was a Boy Scout when I left California. In New York, the Boy Scouts got together in my neighborhood at the old 34th Street Armory on Park Avenue. I went to the first meeting, but thought, "This isn't Boy Scouts, this is a classroom." And that was it for me with Scouting. After that, I was in the Frick Collection or headed up to the Cloisters or something.

Those experiences are the two major components of my early life. One was a very good education, with an exposure both in the States and Europe to a lot of art and architecture, to history and languages and theater. The other was the exposure I had to the natural world in California, a hunger I had then that was almost manic. It's those two elements that so often come together in my work. I believe the environment, the landscape itself, the color and shape and line around you, affects you emotionally. It creates a context for human drama. A lot of that context is physical, of course, but it is also psychological. In *Moby-Dick* you need that big horizon in order for the moral drama to reverberate. There's a strain in American literature that insists on the relevancy of setting. Think about Stephen Crane's "The Open Boat." It's a distinctly American story. Moral drama in an American space. Like Faulkner or Whitman. My roots, I think, are with people like Cather and Steinbeck, writers who were concerned with the role landscape played in the unfolding of human life. They were both aware, as Peter Matthiessen is, as Stegner and Wendell Berry are, that generation just ahead of me, with the convergence of nature and culture. It's a very long list in American letters, from Melville to Cormac McCarthy. When I sit down to write an essay, I'm trying to illuminate an idea as I have encountered it in a physical place, its reification. Here are these ideas—dignity, divinity, integrity—and here are those ideas unfolding in the Arctic, say. That's a lot of what nonfiction is for me.

As a fiction writer, my approach to making a story—to trying to make something beautiful—is different. I have no point I want to make in a story. I am after something closely defined but ineffable. In "The Woman Who Had Shells" [in *Winter Count*], a man is leaving a woman's apartment and she stops him at the door. It came into my conscious mind then, a little bit, "Oh, don't do this, don't go to bed with him." I was resisting it. Sometimes the character knows, and in that sense I'm not able to control the story, to steer it toward a point. I don't have the same degree of control over the narrative in fiction that I do when I'm writing an essay.

Newell: Do you write poetry?

Lopez: I have tried, but it's just beyond me to write a really strong poem. I'm somebody who loves language, who is conscious of rhythm, of assonance and consonance, of the music of language, but I'm a prose writer, not a poet. The density of imagery and the care I take with language sometimes reminds people of the density of imagery and the care with language that are characteristic of poetry, but I have no gift for concision, and I am too strongly wedded to narrative, to be called a poet.

Newell: Prose poetry, would you be comfortable with that, or is that a no-man's land?

Lopez: No, my insistence is that I'm a prose writer. And someone who wants great care with language to also be a distinguishing characteristic of prose.

Newell: Your nonfiction speaks to a certain audience and some of your fiction to that same audience, but some of your fiction is for another audience. Would you agree?

Lopez: You know, I never think about audience. I believe the people who read my work, who might be drawn to it, are curious, they take life seriously, and they want to be reminded of their passion, of the possibilities in their lives. I hope somebody walks away from a story of mine with a larger sense, a clearer sense, of their own possibility.

Newell: Yes, I see that.

Lopez: In "Light Action in the Caribbean," you know, this
fatuous couple is on vacation. As a reader, you're
thinking "Well, these self-important, oblivious people
are making fools of themselves." You like watching it,
because they're inane. And then they're both brutally
murdered by three psychopaths, who come almost
literally out of nowhere. So, someone you had just
been condescending toward is suddenly dead. It
leaves the roots of compassion twisted. Modern
times. Writing those kinds of stories now, it makes
me a little afraid. Anxious. But, as I said, I want to go
after more complex emotions, and I don't imagine
this has to mean a change of audience.

Many years ago I read a review of *Arctic Dreams*
in which the reviewer said, "Lopez is telling us all
about the epistemology of native people, but he's not
telling us about the drunks." I felt like saying, "How
can you have missed the drunkenness, the social disintegration in every indigenous village of the world?
That's the constant refrain. I'm writing the other
story, and I expect you to bring that knowledge of
darkness with you to the other story. If you don't,
what I'm writing could seem sentimental and I'm
not writing sentimentality. I'm offering you, as a
writer with his *own* awareness of darkness, something
to hold against the dark, a plausible light."

What Percival accomplishes in the Grail legend is
to convince us of the existence of light in the same
moment that we are fully aware of darkness. Maybe
what's happening in my prose now, in my fiction, is
that I'm trying to find a way to bring light out of
darkness in a more explicit rather than implicit way.

Newell: You have intent as a nonfiction writer, I sense that.
What do you mean when you say that in fiction, to

some degree, you have no control?

Lopez: If you try to control the story, you can sometimes slide into a dishonest relationship with the reader. I don't want to beat this to death, but I think we've lost our sense in this country that a story represents a relationship between a reader and a writer or a listener and a storyteller. Yes, the work is driven by an artistic vision, and yes, you are writing in solitude, but the impulse to write, I believe, is a social impulse. It's an ethical act. To be inconsiderate of the reader is to capitulate—maybe my view is too extreme, but bear with me—is to capitulate to a crippling belief we have in the cultural West in the primary importance of the individual. We adhere to this view because it's what capitalism feeds on, and capitalism, of course, is what many if not most of us depend on for a livelihood. You can't have capitalism without social disintegration, without pulling the individual out of his social context. Unless you have families falling apart all the time, you can't move the goods and services to make our economy run the way it's supposed to run. Where we're actually headed as a country is not toward greater freedom for the individual, but toward the isolation of the individual. An individual is not isolated if she or he shares. If someone is in a reciprocal relationship, if someone is really "in love"—romantic love or sexual love or platonic love, whatever the adjective is going to be—that's a reciprocal relationship, and it's anathema to the subdivisions in society that capitalism requires to keep itself in prime health.

I'm going too fast here, perhaps a bit of a rant, so let me see if I can make this tighter. One goal capitalism has to have to sustain its growth is the

courtship of people who prefer relationships with
things to relationships with people. This is the loneliness of material existence. The great longing in
American culture is not for things but for friendship.
For simple access to a dependable and understanding
heart. The origin of story in human society, as I
understand it, is exactly there, the effort to place or
replace the individual within the sustaining structure
of a set of relationships—inside a community. It
serves as an antidote to feelings of isolation—of fail-
ure, of shame. Stories, I think, do not so much
instruct as reinforce in us, or revive in us, what we
already know but have forgotten.

Newell: Some stories reveal something that can't be explained
directly. We learn about an indirect connection, arrive
at an inference. We come to a sense of responsibility,
based on what we have gathered from the story. The
experience is synergistic.

Lopez: Sometimes I think of a story as an ecosystem. Sitting
here, on the banks of the [McKenzie] river, the two
of us, we can talk about the patterns around us from
a biological or an aesthetic perspective. We can
watch osprey hunt for trout here, and say, "Well, this
is an example of a predator-prey relationship." Or we
could go into the woods, and see all the mushrooms
erupting there now, and talk about saprophytic food
chains. Talk about the relationships that become
apparent to us, and not dwell on the things, the
objects, in them. The landscape surrounding us contains a set of relationships that can become, through
the structure of a story, like an ecosystem in our
minds. The land then serves a metaphorical purpose.

A lot of what is here in front of us is too subtle to
have a name. The same is true of a story. You say,

"Well, these characters have this kind of relationship," and you elaborate on it. But maybe there's an adjective in the first sentence of a paragraph that's slightly prominent. It has some kind of weight, and it sinks through the entire paragraph. Its influence is felt throughout the paragraph. At the end of the paragraph, there's something going on you can't put your finger on. The word has fallen all the way through to inform the end of the paragraph. It's very subtle. A stone sinking through the currents of the river here, starting with the "plop" that gains your attention. When you make a beautiful story, you in effect make a beautiful small, intricate ecosystem. If a person comes to that story feeling a little bit disaffected, say, and reads the story and puts the book down, and feels refreshed, I think what's happening is that this little ecosystem on the page has gotten inside the person and rearranged his emotions, and now he feels whole, he feels integrated, he feels good relationships inside himself. It's almost a physical feeling. In that sense you can say, for a particular person at a particular moment, a story is inspiring, not because the story necessarily has something wise to say, but because the relationships are beautiful. It makes it possible to turn to your spouse, turn to your children, turn to your parents and say, "I love you," and there's no string in it. It's in this way that story is therapeutic. And I believe that has been the case with story from the beginning.

Making a story is so commercialized now. It's a creation for sale. We've lost the sense of story as a gift. It's story as commodity. Every writer today I think struggles in that middle ground. You know what's coming through you is a gift, and when it goes down on the page and is given to somebody, that's a continuation of the gift. Somewhere in your psyche as a writer, you question how you can actually be making your living as a writer. It doesn't feel quite right, somehow. The work is not entirely yours. All the images, all the imagination, all that's yours; but there's something else going on that's not yours to sell. If you lean too far into that place where the story is a commodity, something for sale, that's when you start writing commercial prose. A reader closes that kind of book and says, "Why did I pay $24.95 for this?" It feels like a stunt. The impact doesn't last. You don't even remember it.

Newell: There are many books out there like that now. Do you think there are still a lot of good writers?

Lopez: Yes. I'm surprised, really, by how many good things I find. I read, like all writers do. I pick up things all over the place, and my sense that writing is in good shape is often renewed. So many men and women whose names you don't know—because the machinery of publicity hasn't caught up with them—are writing these tender, wise, beautiful stories.

Newell: Is there a novel in you?

Lopez: Yes.

Newell: Is it coming?

Lopez: It'll come along. Right now I see a convergence in my work. If you put *Winter Count* here and *Of Wolves and Men* over here, and looked at how those fiction and nonfiction paths might converge, I believe that's how this large-scale book I'm working on will open up.

Newell: Is this large-scale book something that you have a handle on now or is this something—

Lopez: Yes, I do. I've just not been able to get to it. As you grow older your writing life gets denser with unfinished projects and distractions. I could spend every day just dealing with the *business* that a life of writing creates. Translations, for example. This isn't to complain. I'm just saying that the time to write was all over the place when I was twenty-three and, now....

Newell: You have a way in much of your work of slowing the reader down, of asking for an attentiveness to every word.

Lopez: Yes, I do. I don't often do it consciously, deliberately, I just move slowly in a story. A friend of mine, a writer, once said, "I read these stories in *Field Notes* when they came out. They were beautiful. Then I read the book again and realized I hadn't really read it. I was so busy moving through the book I never looked down, I never saw what was going on underneath. It was the difference between crossing a river on the ice, an intensely beautiful scene, and being propelled through that world, and, the second time, looking down through the clear ice at the moving river." I'd like to think that you can read the surface of my stories, and that they make engaging sense that way. But for the reader who is pausing, I hope to have more. I believe I learned this "pausing" from Hopkins, from Gerard Manley Hopkins, probably the first poet that made me acutely aware of meter. I know that there is meter in my prose, and that I use it to do a number of things, including creating rhythms that ask you to pause.

Newell: What are some of those other techniques?

Lopez: I use meter to accentuate parts of a paragraph. I use meter for punctuation. A good example of that is in an essay called, "The American Geographies." There's a very long sentence in there, several hundred words long. Whenever that piece gets reprinted, a copy editor will tell me they have to punctuate it. I say, "Why?" and they say, "It's so long." I say, "Did you not understand it, did you get lost in it?" "No." "Why do you have to punctuate it, then?" "Well, because it's so long." Well, you punctuate to clarify, not because things are "too long." I can show you the sentence [pages through *About This Life*].

Newell: You know, I picked up a master's in Environmental Law from Vermont Law School and I read Supreme Court decisions with long, long sentences that were very clear.

Lopez: Yes, some nineteenth-century legal opinions are unbelievably well-written. I actually talked to Sandra Day O'Connor at a dinner once about this. She said that, by comparison, Supreme Court opinions today are turgid, convoluted, and sometimes vague. But there is a grace in some of that earlier work where the justices really took the writing seriously.

Newell: It was as if they did something in their writing that let you see into their minds. I would say that meter played a role in how they packaged their decisions.

Lopez: [Points out long sentence in "The American Geographies."] That's it [on page 140]. There's nothing but commas. What [copy editors] usually try to do is substitute semicolons. It's the meter that carries it. You're so clearly moving across the U.S. from east to west in this sentence, anyone with some remnant of a U.S. map floating around in their head knows where we're going.

Newell: Well, you see, your readers can't escape either. Your readers can't "chunk" [speed read]—I'm a reading teacher by training—you can't chunk it, you can't predict it because it's not predictable. If you try to do speed reading with *your* writing, then you miss the sublime, the pulse beneath the skin.

Lopez: Well, I'm getting a lot of credit here for something I don't understand all that well.

Newell: In my mind the duty of the reader is to read every word, to let it all unfold in its own time. Otherwise you miss what's brewing within the syllables themselves.

Lopez: Someone once asked Bob Stone what sort of reader he imagined as an ideal. He said, "You hope for someone who reads as carefully as you write." Much of the rewriting I do—I take most pieces through four or five drafts—is trying to make the rhythm inform the meaning of the sentences, and finding more concise ways, more elegant ways to say something, or adding connective tissue when I realize the leap from one paragraph to another is too great. If I see a phrase in my nonfiction prose, like "But to return to the subject," or "As I was saying," or "Now, I would like to talk about," I know I've given the reader a poor map and I need to make a better one. Inevitably, phrases like those are going to turn up— I'm sure they're there in my work—but my goal is to get you from the beginning to the end of the story *in the story*, not by standing apart from it and giving you directions about where to go.

I'm not a writer who experiments very much, but in a story called "Death," at the end of *About This Life*, I was trying to evoke an emotion by creating scenes that were not tied together. A few references tie the beginning and the end together, but the breaks between the other sections are abrupt. There's a complete change of venue. I did this intentionally in a story called "The Construction of the *Rachel*" [in *Light Action in the Caribbean*]. The narrator is sitting beside a pool in a hotel in Nevada one evening, reading a book. He's reading and he looks up and thinks of something not connected to what's going on in the book, but which is emotionally connected to his experience of *reading* that book. When he looks up, he sees a monk attending to a lost child in a cloister, in a monastery, and that's where that section ends. The next sentence, which begins a new section, assumes you know we are now in a monastery. It's a kind of transition I discovered while writing a memoir, but it interested me enough to employ it consciously as a technique in a work of fiction three years later.

Newell: You trust the reader.

Lopez: Yeah, I do. I trust that if the reader feels like a companion, he or she will move easily through such transitions, and that part of the pleasure a person takes in reading is in being treated that way, treated as though their own imagination was integral to the working of the story. If you don't bring your own imagination to a story I've written, it's not going to work very well.

Newell: Well, you know, that respect for the reader is probably... that's an interesting concept. If you look at the prose of a hundred years ago or fifty years ago, it's death for a teacher to give it to teenagers, because often times the reader isn't trusted. The reader is taken through a lot of character and plot development in baby steps. It's tough for kids to hang onto. The underlying stylistic issues are complex, to be sure, but a lot of the writing of a hundred years ago or fifty years ago didn't show much respect for the reader's intelligence or imagination. Do you differ with that?

Lopez: I don't know. I've been strongly influenced as a storyteller by contact with native peoples. A Métis man told me once, when I asked him how he imagined storytellers fit into his society, "You're the storyteller as long as the stories that you tell help. When they don't help anymore, you're not the storyteller, even if you say you are." To put this maybe too succinctly, I would say that what I'm trying to do is write stories that help, and part of doing that is making a respectful approach to the reader. Several people, I suspect for very different reasons, have said that my fiction reminds them of Henry James, which I never would have said myself. I don't quite know what they mean by that; but one person clarified by saying, "There is more going on in the few pages of a short story of yours than is going on in most novels." But what's essential to remember here is that whatever is going on, it involves two people, the reader and the writer.

Newell: Sometimes dealing with a piece of yours takes up a lot of memory, so to speak, to use computer jargon. It's a signature of yours.

Lopez: When Russell Banks heard me read "The Letters of Heaven" he came up and hugged me and he said, "It's such a pleasure to hear a writer who's not afraid to think." I have great admiration for Russell. I see him as a writer senior to me, as much as I feel I'm his colleague, because he knows way more than I do about fiction. I told him once that I was more interested in being the reader's companion than the reader's authority, and he said that's exactly how he saw himself, as the reader's companion.

Newell: You said earlier that Banks understood your first-person narrators in fiction as characters—that we were in their world, not Barry's world.

Lopez: This new collection of stories, *Light Action in the*

Caribbean, has about sixteen stories in it at the moment. Probably thirteen of them are told by first-person narrators, but they're all different people. I don't reflect on this very much, but it obviously helps some people if they understand that *River Notes*—to reach way back here—is not an autobiographical book, and that this statement, that it and the other story collections are not autobiographical, is not an effort to forestall an inquiry into my private life. It's a statement about narrative technique.

Newell: You lure the reader in that way. That reaching for intimacy with the reader, coupled with so much specific detail in your stories, in my mind, is what lures the reader in.

Lopez: So does the use of the present tense, which I favor. A successful story, in fiction or nonfiction, has to balance the particular against the general. There has to be a certain kind of particularity in order to make a general statement ring true. In a story called "The Mappist" [in *Light Action in the Caribbean*], a man is trying to track down a person he finally meets at the end of the story. The key to his search comes in a bookstore in Jimbocho, in Chiyoda-ku, a part of Tokyo. When I was writing the story, I wanted to be very precise about where this bookstore was, but in rewriting it, I went through and struck out some of the language because its precision was appropriate only to nonfiction. It was one detail too many for fiction.

Newell: Of course this bookstore doesn't exist.

Lopez: Actually, it does [laughs]. And that night when I went to bed, I remember looking at that paragraph in my mind, seeing that the rhythm would be better if one of those particularizing pieces of information I'd left in went into the *second* of the first two sentences.

Newell: You pay attention to your sentences like poets pay attention.

Lopez: Well, you're giving me a lot of credit here—or maybe *I'm* giving myself a lot of credit—for what is just obsessiveness. And I should say that it's sometimes been editors who've helped me to say better what I'm trying to say. They've clarified something I couldn't see, and so pointed me toward some change that made the story work better. I'm thinking of two instances. One was Janet Wondra, some years ago, at *The Georgia Review.* She made a single remark about the narrator in "The Letters of Heaven" that showed me how to recast a couple of sentences that greatly improved the story. "Ramon [the narrator]," she said, "is a man who lives in his head, and he's reading the letters of heaven as literature." I thought, "Yes, and that means he's also trying to get *out* of his head." That single remark might have generated the sentence in which Ramon tells us his wife had become almost an idea to him. Suddenly, because of Janet, I understood something. Lois Rosenthal, when she was the editor of *Story*, told me, when she read "The Deaf Girl," that she got side-tracked at the beginning because she thought, "How can somebody with a bullet in their head be coherent?" She said, "I don't know anything about ballistics, but is it possible for somebody to be shot in the head and to walk along like this and carry on a conversation? It was so distracting, it pulled me away from the story." I said, "Well, no, I didn't think about that. I assumed most people would understand that the bullet just grazed her head." Lois said, "Well, it would help me a lot if you would be explicit about that." So I did. I changed the clause in the sentence to make it more explicit that she was grazed by the bullet.

Newell: Before her comment, had you used the word "grazed"?

Lopez: No. Lois said, "Well, do you get a lot of blood from a head wound?" I said, "Yes, eighteen percent of a person's blood flow is to the head. A head wound bleeds like crazy." There's much less blood going into an arm, say, than is going into the head. This is a matter of being correct in fiction about a matter of fact. But Lois was correct, too, saying you're running the risk of having the reader fall out of the story, thinking, "Gosh, how can this little girl be functioning?" Toby Wolff took a story of mine when he was editing an anthology, and said "I don't think this ending works as well as you want it to work. It's not a big deal to me if you don't want to change it. It's okay with me, but I really think you need to look at how this story ends." I did, and I decided that I didn't need to change it. I have such respect for Toby, though, that I tried to figure out how to make it work in such a way that Toby would feel more comfortable with it. I finally told him, "I think the narrator uses a few locutions at the end here that are peculiar to his dialect. I could change them but then it wouldn't be his language anymore." This was just a place where two writers had different points of view.

Newell: I'm thinking about "The Deaf Girl." It can be maddening to be left not knowing what that deaf girl did to the rapist, but it would take away from the story, I think, to know that.

Lopez: I got a letter from a guy—I think he missed something in "The Deaf Girl"—he said, "You've got this story wrong. You need to rewrite this and tell us how she

confronted this guy," and we need to know more
about this, that, and so on. I wrote him back and said
as politely as I could, "Well, the story is not about her."

Newell: That's right. It's *not* about her.

Lopez: It's about a man who is comfortable in his life. The
girl says to him, in effect, "There's no reason for you
to be comfortable. There is something missing in you,
and you need to go and discover it." When she goes
off and he realizes she's not going to go kill the boy,
he has his work cut out for him.

Newell: I like that the narrator in "Sonora" [in *Field Notes*]
is also deaf. These characters really listen, but not
with their ears. Let me change subjects and ask
whether you're involved in very many projects that
have remained obscure, that you think people don't
know about.

Lopez: I'm always talking with other artists about collaboration. A friend of mine, Dick Nelson, wrote a book
called *Make Prayers to the Raven*. When he got the
money to do a five-part series for television, he asked
if I would do the narration and I said yes. Since then,
the series has aired repeatedly in the U.S. and
Canada. I'm almost always at work with book artists
and with designers at small presses on limited edition
books. I often work with John Luther Adams, the
composer. These are just endeavors or projects that
are exciting for me to be involved with. Books-on-
tape. The books-on-tape version of *About This Life*
was a finalist for an Audi Award, which is like an
Emmy for spoken language. I like trying to make
beautiful things with other people. You can lose that
overly-romanticized sense of being a lone outrider
telling civilization what it needs to know. You
become just another voice in the chorus. In ensemble

work in the theater, in collaboration with a musician, you create a short-lived community, and that kind of creation interests me. Manfred Eicher, the producer at ECM Records who's brought out so many singular musicians and artists—Keith Jarrett, the Hilliard Ensemble, Gavin Bryars—came to me and asked if I'd think about an alternative to liner notes. I'd actually been thinking about that, about writing a short story in emotional parallel to the development of a piece of music. I asked him to send me, with no language, no titles, no descriptive material of any sort, a CD and let me respond to it. All I needed to know was the order the pieces would occur in, so I could write a story that would parallel that progression. We put the story in the CD [*Dark Wood*, David Darling, cellist] and left entirely in the listeners'/readers' hands the decision about how the story and the music are related.

Newell: That's kind of a twist. Usually the music follows from the words.

Lopez: I imagine every story in a way similar to the way a composer imagines a sonata, I think. It's entire unto itself. It's a piece of cloth, taken from your experience of the world. Tearing it out leaves a hole in your experience, and you're faced with the rough edges of the tear, but I want that whole piece of cloth. I see it as an organic entity, each of its parts in relation to the others, the way parts of an ecosystem relate.

Another way a story often develops for me is to have a first line that triggers everything. I'll hear it and then I can't get it out of my mind until I write the story. "Stolen Horses" [in *Light Action in the Caribbean*] was like that. I just kept hearing that line, "What we did was wrong, of course...." Or I think I told you about starting with an image, in "The Deaf Girl." I saw this child in a black frock, walking on a hillside. With "Empira's Tapestry" [in *Field Notes*] I had the memory of an image that came to me walking in the woods once, where I just looked up and saw a woman from the back, making this gesture of comfort and reassurance with two children. Then she pulled a cloak around herself and turned and I lost it. I lost what I was imagining. I had that idea in my head, that image, though, for a long time. One day I pulled on it and found that the memory had accreted to itself—in the way an irritating grain of sand accretes to itself and we get a pearl—had accreted to itself other images. When I pulled on it, another image came, and another, everything that had become attached to it over time. It was a string winding through my imagination, and it had drawn to itself all that it was attracted to. When I pulled on it, it came out whole.

Newell: Empira is not physically attractive—

Lopez: No.

Newell: —and for me is an example of these obscure but exemplary individuals you write about. She's one of those beautiful creatures that we miss because of our first impressions.

Lopez: I want the stories and essays to be, I guess, a reminder—to borrow one of your expressions—of the "divine interior" of the ordinary event or the ordinary person.

Newell: There's a style in your earlier work, *Desert Notes* especially, and *River Notes,* it's a little surreal, it doesn't quite mesh. Some endings even seem tagged on, but it's like you're trying to accomplish something, a style you're trying to find your way to.

Lopez: People argue whether *Desert Notes* and *River Notes* are fiction or not. I wrote them as fiction. We're in a world of first-person narrators who aren't me and most of what is described is made up—the events, not the settings. I can understand, if you're a reader who comes to those books from *Crossing Open Ground* or *Of Wolves and Men*, that you're not prepared to approach them in a neutral way. It irritates me, though, that somebody can't tell the difference between the "I" of an essay and the "I" of a story. In those early stories, which may not be as skillfully written as later work, you're right, though. I'm trying to find a way to tell a "true" story that is not in the manner of nonfiction.

I got a letter once from a reader, right after *Desert Notes* came out, who said Borges influence on my work was clear. At the time I didn't know who Borges was. I didn't know his work at all. Then, probably a year later, I began reading Borges, and I thought, "Oh, I see what this person meant." Someone who believes all work is derivative, that I had read Borges, for example, and was trying to work in that vein, is usually someone I can't have much of a conversation with. The trouble with using a term like "magical realism" to describe someone's work is that it sounds as though somebody invented a formula, and then others began working with the formula. What I think happens is that a number of writers discover for themselves the same way of working. It's interesting and satisfying. Exciting. After a while, somebody on the outside notices these writers have something in common, and they give that technique or style a name. If you come along after the style has been named, in the case of *Desert Notes* and *River*

Notes, magical realism, *lo real maravilloso* in Spanish, if you come to that discovery for yourself, after the term has been invented, some people assume you've been reading other people's work. It's not always the case.

Newell: Most writers find their own way.

Lopez: You do if you're a writer. If you just want to be well known, if all you're really after is a large reputation, well then, you might try imitating what's out there that's generating a buzz. Editors at literary magazines have told me that as soon as a writer becomes hot, the magazines are flooded with imitations of their work. Ray Carver comes into prominence and all of a sudden these editors see hundreds of Carver-like submissions.

Newell: That makes perfect sense. I asked you earlier about finding current writers out there who are good—and original. How do you find them?

Lopez: The same way you do, I imagine. You're in a bookstore, you pick something up, or something comes in the mail, or somebody leaves a book behind at your house. Sometimes you get good recommendations from friends. I remember in 1985 Dan Halpern, the publisher and poet, asked me if I had ever read Cormac McCarthy. At the time I hadn't. Now I go to new work of his immediately. I'm pretty sure it was also Dan Halpern who recommended another writer I've become very fond of, an English novelist named Jim Crace—

Newell: *The Gift of Stones*—

Lopez: *Gift of Stones*, *Signals of Distress*, *Quarantine*, *Continent*—

Newell: Bruce Chatwin, you know, similar—

Lopez: I remember when Chatwin died, I waded out into the river here and began to cry. I felt the loss was so great. The novelist Howard Norman was the first person to recommend him to me. Chatwin and I had some friends in common in Australia then—

Newell: Oh, *Songlines*—

Lopez: —but I had some very strong disagreements with him about fiction and nonfiction. Not so much with *Songlines* but with the way *In Patagonia* masquerades as a work of nonfiction when it's full of things he made up. Writers in England have described my work—or me—as an American version of Bruce Chatwin. I would say that's simply inaccurate, because I'm so strict about the differences between fiction and nonfiction. I think the relationship Chatwin had with the reader was informed in a different way than mine is. Two biographies have come out in the last two years. I've read one. The other one might be even more informing about the way he chose to blend fiction and nonfiction.

Newell: The surreal stretching in some of your earlier work comes together for me in your later work, especially well with *Winter Count*. But some reviewers have said it was *Of Wolves and Men* that pulled you together as a writer. Would you agree with that?

Lopez: Maybe it pulled a certain part of my work together. It was the first large-scale nonfiction project, and it required a lot of field work and library work. In *Winter Count* I might have achieved something I had been trying to accomplish in *Desert Notes* and in *River Notes*. Even when I got into that long nonfiction period in the eighties, though, I was still yearning to return to a process of discovery in fiction. The first time I did was with *Crow and Weasel* and that's why I say that *Field Notes* has more in common with *Winter Count* than it does with *Desert Notes* and *River Notes*. It's more accomplished. I have to say, though, there is an aspect of *Desert Notes* and *River Notes* that I could not capture now, some combination of innocence and unselfconsciousness. And there are stories in *Winter Count* that I couldn't write today—"The Woman Who Had Shells," for example. I don't have the naïveté.

I'm glad those books [*Desert Notes* and *River Notes*] were published early because, after *Winter Count* came out, the temptation would have been to rewrite those manuscripts. It would have made them much less interesting books, I think. *Desert Notes* and *River Notes* are an effort to explore landscape in a fictive way. I'd much rather do something like that and fail at it than do something that has been done well before and do it well. I think that's a pattern in my work, that I start out with something I don't really understand and then just work at it until it gets better, until I get better at it. I like to push. I like to refine. I like the risk, you know, in pushing compassion right to the edge of sentimentality. If I look back over my nonfiction and then look at what I'm trying to do in nonfiction now, the phrase that comes to me is "working without a net."

Newell: The net being what?

Lopez: Authority. What happens in nonfiction when you don't rely primarily on the authority of other voices? You have to in reporting, in journalism. You customarily do in an essay, less so in the "personal essay" I suppose. And then, in nonfiction, we enter the realm of the memoir, where the writer is his or her own authority. The question I am pursuing now I guess is how to combine the authority of the self with the authority of the world beyond the self. How can you occupy the shared world, the historical world, and, at the same time, the personal world and still gain the reader's trust? This is an impenetrable problem for me right now. It's always there, right at the edge of my thoughts. I don't think about it very much, but it dogs me.

Newell: I want to get back to your fiction for a moment. First, where does the collection of trickster stories, *Giving Birth to Thunder*, fit in the development of your fiction, and what was your going to Galisteo, New Mexico, recently all about?

Lopez: *Giving Birth to Thunder* starts with Barre Toelken. He was an English professor at the University of Oregon when I was there in '68 and '69. It's in his folklore classes that I first became acquainted with the trickster figure, whom Jung characterized as "a creature of undifferentiated good and evil," a Paleolithic persona, found in traditional stories all over the world. I began reading stories of his North American incarnations in *The Journal of American Folklore*, in the Bureau of American Ethnology *Bulletins* and *Reports*, in the papers of the Jessup Expedition, and other scholarly and academic publications. When I read Paul Radin and Jaime de Angulo and others on the character— and talked with Barre, who'd married into a Navajo family—I began to think the stories could be presented in a more vernacular way, and that they would then appeal, like the trickster figure Randall McMurphy in Kesey's *Sometimes a Great Notion*, to a wider audience. I finally brought together about sixty stories, from many different North American traditions, in a kind of cycle. Barre wrote a foreword, which was more generous and gracious of him than I was able to grasp at the time. I wrote an introduction about my research and methods, and a narrative bibliography. I got a crack across the knuckles from a couple of academics, for what they saw as trespassing in their discipline, but, as I recall, the book was well received by native people and general readers. Toelken was at a gathering somewhere once, and had a copy of *Giving Birth to Thunder* under his arm when he walked into a conference room. A Nez Perce man saw the book and said, "What's this? Another white guy writing about Indian life?" Barre didn't know what to say. The guy walked away with the book, really irritated, a kind of chip on his shoulder. That evening he gave the book back to Barre and said, "This is exactly how my dad used to tell the stories," and walked away. What I didn't know when I was writing the book was that Toelken, who was one of the founders of Native American studies, along with people like Joe Brown at Montana, had an unimpeachable reputation among native people. By putting his name on the book he was vouching for me. Barre opened many doors into the Indian community for me when I was in my early twenties. He had a profound influence on my work.

Newell: And Galisteo?

Lopez: I don't know what happened there. I just seemed to work really well in circumstances that were new for me. The stories I wrote there [four appear in *Light Action in the Caribbean*] don't have to do with that part of New Mexico. One is set in North Dakota, another in California, another in Syria, a fourth in the Caribbean, another in Nags Head, on the North Carolina coast, and one has no real setting. It comes to a head in a hotel in Milan.

Newell: So the conduciveness of the place...

Lopez: It was the quietness, an adobe house with stone floors, set within an enclosure of adobe walls, cottonwoods, horses grazing beyond, dogs asleep in the dirt streets, a lot of sunlight. It was an archetypal place for me.

Newell: Had you written there before?

Lopez: I'd never been there. I wanted to spend a couple of weeks isolated and writing in New Mexico. I called someone at the Lannan Foundation in Santa Fe and asked if they knew of any houses down there that I could stay at. They said, "We just bought a house nearby, in a small village called Galisteo. Let us know what you're doing, it might be the sort of thing we'd support." I sent them an outline of the work and some dates and I got a nice letter back and went right down.

Newell: That is interesting. You'll go back there, then?

Lopez: I will. Bernard Pomerance, who wrote *The Elephant Man*, lives just down the road. We enjoy visiting. A woman who had a very strong influence on my life, a painter named Sue Hertel, used to live nearby. She died a few years ago of cancer, but I visit her daughter now on her ranch. A couple of friends live there. John Flax, the artistic director of Theater Grottesco, Tom Joyce, an artist and blacksmith, Lucy Lippard, the art critic. The landscape itself... I can't imagine a place more conducive for me. Everywhere I went during those weeks—this is almost eerie—people who didn't know me took me for someone local.

Newell: That's always a compliment.

Lopez: For thirty years virtually everything I'd written I'd written in my house. That was the first time I went away from home and wrote. It didn't seem like I was trying anything new, I just wanted to get inside a quieter place. Even with my reclusive life here, I feel constant interruption, mail and phone calls, the interminable paper work you're obliged to deal with as a writer. I sound like I'm complaining, but I'm trying to get at something important here. When I was a child in California I lived in a sexually abusive situation with a man who insinuated himself into our family after my father walked out on us, walked out on my younger brother, my mother, and me. Many situations like this are so insidious you can't deal with them, let alone understand them in the moment, and this went on for years. Whenever I could escape it, whenever I could get away into the Mojave Desert or into the mountains or the Grand Canyon, the relief I felt was extraordinary. Not to be afraid for a few days, not to be cornered every other night by someone. Going to New Mexico to write, in a deeply peaceful house behind adobe walls, the beautiful desert light, wind rustling in the crowns of cottonwoods in the bosque behind the house. To have that and with it only the self-imposed responsibility of making stories, it is so very, very different from the life most of us, myself included, are required to live most of the time, accommodating ourselves to the world's intrusions, the inquiries of strangers.

The rental cabin where the conversations took place.

Now known as North, Middle and South Peaks in the Three Sisters Wilderness Area, these volcanic mountains were called Mount Faith, Mount Hope and Mount Charity by Methodist missionaries in the 1840s.

Barry Lopez shows the author a Pacific madrone.

Two views of the bridge from "The Log Jam"—the top deck...

...and from the water line.

The author reading on the cabin's back deck, beside the timpanic McKenzie.

In between taking photographs, Phyllis reads an issue of *Story*
that Barry provided.

Dr. Patrick Meanor and Barry Lopez at the State University of New York at Oneonta Mills Lecture Series, October 2002.

A Critical Discussion:
The Short Story Books

Introduction

Barry Lopez is a wordsmith. For decades he has moved deftly among writing genres, becoming fluent within their distinctive techniques. This dexterity enables his fiction to appear all the more authentic. By using a tone and rhythm normally associated with nonfiction or a formal argument, Lopez spins fictive truths new readers passionately argue must be factual. Truthful these yarns often are—but only in the magical realm of storytelling. Told primarily in the first person and with most characters lacking names, the earliest short stories can cause the unwary reader to believe them to be autobiographical. Russell Banks once warned Lopez that this Victorian style would likely confuse the contemporary reader. He said, "You use non-autobiographical, 19th-century, first-person narrators, but today the first person sends signals about autobiography, that the story is about you." As for the lack of usual background information surrounding the protagonists in his earlier fiction, Lopez told this writer, "Early on, I wanted to protect even the privacy of my characters."

Some readers may suspect a contradiction in Lopez's penchant for his stylistic technique of keeping his private life at arm's length from his fictive prose. To be sure, vestigial elements of his youth have informed and enhanced his fiction, i.e., a Roman Catholic, Jesuit upbringing. There is also his affinity for the natural world, marginalized cultures and Trickster figures. As the narrator mused in *Winter Count*'s "The Tapestry," "It is by such early, seemingly inconsequential and innocent passions, of course, that we are formed." Readers should not confuse privacy with secrecy. Those who are curious for autobiographical material will be delighted upon reading his nonfiction, including *Arctic Dreams* and *About This Life.*

Lopez's short stories engage and "reinforce in us, or revive in us, what we already know but have forgotten." He is a master storyteller in the classical tradition of being a companion to the reader. Even the playfulness of the earliest stories arouses a reader's sense of community toward his home ground and his neighbors. Hallmarks of his themes and style are embryonic in the early short stories: koans, instructions, purification/novitiate rituals, patience, attentiveness, understatement and a deliberate lack of closure. Collectively, his protagonists' self-absorptions yield to self-knowledge and provide what Lopez has described as learning what it is that one means. Readers should be cautioned. Those who venture into his imaginative landscapes risk a shedding of cultural baggage, a livelier step and an expansive mien.

I began researching and collecting material for this section in 1999, prior to our conversations in Oregon and continuing through the typesetting for *No Bottom.* Lopez and I corresponded on all his short story books except *Resistance.* He generously provided me with materials and information designed to heighten the article's technical, chronological and biographical accuracy. However, all critical connections, observations and interpretations are solely my own and in no way represent his endorsement.

Although the basic premises from my original manuscript have remained intact, this current version has made way for ideas engendered by *Resistance,* by a bevy of other writers' interviews with Lopez since 2001, by archival references available online, by newly minted journal articles, by his regularly updated website, by more recent correspondences and conversations we shared and by public presentations of his which I attended.

What follows is a literary biography that focuses on Barry Lopez's short story books: *Desert Notes, River Notes, Winter Count, Field Notes, Light Action in the Caribbean,* and *Resistance.* Seminal works, especially in his nonfiction, are alluded to. For readers who might question why the more traditional term of short story "collections" isn't adopted, it might be useful to know that Lopez believes the stories have the collective impact associated with a book. He purposefully selects and choreographs the short story arrangements within each book. Alone, each short story emits its own singular aura. Just as any book's chapters coalesce, the short stories of a particular book by Lopez spill into one another. Within those collective synergies unfold tones and hues that become dreamlike in their truth-lettings. The ensuing critical discussion illustrates other unlikely but imaginative transgenric techniques found throughout his fiction.

The Formative Years

Barry Holstun Lopez was born in Port Chester, New York, on January 6, 1945, to John Edward Brennan and Mary Frances (Holstun) Brennan. Both parents worked in journalism and advertising. Lopez's precocious affinity for landscape revealed itself early on. John Tallmadge, in *American Nature Writers,* wrote that "some of Lopez's earliest landscape memories involve wading into Long Island Sound as a three-year-old, drawn by the light and space out on the water." When Lopez was three his family, including a newborn brother, Dennis, moved to the San Fernando Valley. It was here that Lopez developed an uncanny allegiance to his natural surroundings and was profoundly influenced by the dinner conversations of well-educated, well-traveled guests.

Lopez's Roman Catholic upbringing began in Our Lady

of Grace School for grades 1-6. Divorced in 1950, his mother remarried in 1955 to Adrian Bernard Lopez, a businessman who adopted her sons and developed a significant father-son relationship with Lopez. Upon moving to Manhattan in 1956, Lopez attended Loyola, a private Jesuit school for boys, from grades 7-12. It was here that he traded in his Boy Scout uniform for books, museums and debutante balls. He subsequently became sensitized to intellects who were marginalized due to their minority status.

Upon graduation in 1962, Lopez spent the summer in Europe. He extended his Roman Catholic upbringing by enrolling in the University of Notre Dame in the fall. His first published piece of fiction, written when he was a senior, appeared in *Ave Maria,* a Roman Catholic weekly magazine, in 1966. Portentously enough, "The Gift" explores a constant theme of Lopez's—exploitation of the natural world for selfish gain. An undergraduate major in communication arts allowed him to blend writing, theatre and American studies. Throughout his undergraduate years, he traveled in every state but Oklahoma, Alaska and Hawai'i. Upon receiving an A.B. from the University of Notre Dame in 1966, he considered becoming a monk, visiting the Trappist Abbey of Gethsemane in Kentucky in November.

Resolving to involve himself with the world's affairs, Lopez chose instead to become an "instrument of grace" and pursued teaching. His marriage, in 1967, to Sandra Landers "lasted almost thirty years." He was an H.E.A. Title V Fellow in 1967-68, during which he earned a Master of Arts in teaching from Notre Dame in 1968. Deciding to make his living as a writer and photographer, Lopez then enrolled in the University of Oregon's M.F.A. creative writing program. He soon became disillusioned with the thrust of a program that "had too much of a sense of the writer and not nearly enough sense of the reader." A chance encounter with Barre Toelken, a U. of O. English professor, then propelled Lopez into studies of Native American cultures. Those inquiries provided a grounding. In understanding how closely aligned he was with Native Americans' spiritual affinity for the lands they inhabited, Lopez came to know what he "means" as a writer. Everything else had been in place: a playful imagination, an insatiable curiosity and an utter reverence for the natural world.

His subsequent studies were pivotal in providing a vision and a voice in which to articulate a deeply felt respect for the life-sustaining forces in all landscapes. Folklores connected Lopez's "passion [for] language and landscape, and those two are inseparable for [him)]." Unlike Western man, aboriginal people "did not separate humanity and nature. They recognized the divine in both," he acknowledged.

Giving Birth to Thunder, Sleeping with His Daughter: Coyote Builds North America (1978) became the creative culmination of his studies of Native American cultures. It was the first book that Lopez had *written* and is distinguished from *Desert Notes: Reflections in the Eye of a Raven* (1976) which was the first book he *published*. Jim Andrews, of Andrews & McMeel publishers, "loved the irreverence of *Giving Birth to Thunder,* the risqué humor." Based on the Trickster coyote figure in Native American folklore, *Giving Birth to Thunder* also brought Lopez "more fully into the life of a freelance writer."

From the 1960s onward, he has been a prolific writer. Lopez's literary apprenticeship included boiler-plate how-tos for a medley of technical topics, numerous book reviews, an infrequent movie review, essays with overtones of social conscience, short fiction and stringer articles for major newspapers. Even then, his early work found publication in a myriad of periodicals as diverse in readership as *Popular Mechanics, Reader's Digest, The New York Times, The Washington Post, Outside* and *Northwest Review.* Until he put the camera down for good in 1981, his own photography complemented his writings.

Since 1970, Lopez's home ground has been along the McKenzie River in Oregon, located on "traditional Tsanchifin Kalapuya Land" in the "Cascade Physiographic Province." From that vantage point he ventures into the world, he has observed, like local salmon smolts that descend to the ocean but ultimately return.

A Literary Preamble

Barry Lopez's literary musings describe a literature of hope. They offer respite and reassurance from life's travails. Lopez believes in the time-honored values of stories and of story-telling to inform, to provide inspirational building blocks and to heal. "The impulse to write," he believes, "is a social impulse. It's an ethical act." His stories reaffirm the capacity of humans to lead dignified lives under dark circumstances. His characters, through their collective odysseys, offer light as counterpoint to a spiritual angst that has become a commercial accelerant in Western society.

For Lopez, there is a divine interior within ordinary events. For him, a divine presence, the *numen*, dwells in all natural objects. For solace and affirmation, he returns to the natural world "as the writers of another generation once returned repeatedly to Freud." While there, he is reverently attentive to the multiple, parallel cultures coexisting amongst humans and nonhumans. Such raptness permits him to access trustworthy patterns that illuminate what is required in all cultures to make a worthy life, one that is "led with moral intention." Central to Lopez's writings are physical landscapes and indigenous cultures which inform by their very act of having sustained that which is "fundamental to the spiritual and intellectual and physical health of human beings on the planet."

When Lopez writes of a landscape, even "sounds common to the region" are integrated. His writings examine issues of tolerance, compassion, how local landscapes sustain human beings, as well as contemporary man's uneven quest for spiritual harmony in a Western culture built on hypercapitalism.

For Lopez, the role of the writer is similar to that of an Eskimo *isumataq*, a storyteller who creates the atmosphere in which wisdom reveals itself. Not by appearing all-knowing or artificially wise but by being responsible to the subject matter *and* reader, Lopez believes the writer most aptly fulfills this role. As in Métis society, "You're the storyteller as long as the stories you tell help." To this end, he listens attentively in his travels, which include remote regions of the globe. By abandoning "the security of the familiar," he periodically takes the measure of a metaphor's vitality "to ground the reader in something trustworthy." He explores the exquisite underplay of those cultures only by suspending Aristotelian, Cartesian and Baconian biases and by patiently allowing himself to be tutored at great length by the natural world and non-Western cultures.

Spiritual openness allows Lopez to "honor the unspoken request of our companions to speak the truth." Those spiritually informing companions are not limited to humankind or even to the glamour species in the natural world, such as the whale, the eagle and the wolf. They encompass "Aztecan, Lakotan, lupine, avian or invertebrate" cultures and even extend to space, darkness and silence. At times, the subject matter of his writing has been prescient. Published in 1975, "The Passing of the Night" laments the "the idea of darkness as one more dwindling natural resource." Even in rural America the proliferation of outdoor, artificial lighting pollutes viewsheds of the constellations and other celestial events.

Acknowledging that language is a living entity in which the reader and writer share symbiotic roles, Lopez strives to be the "reader's companion, [rather] than the reader's author-

ity," as Ishmael was the reader's companion in Herman
Melville's *Moby Dick*. Lopez does not want to lead the reader, but rather "to construct something, the story, in which a
number of disparate imaginations can range freely and widely and productively." In pursuing this role, he respectfully
bows first to the material and then to the reader. Once he
establishes trust and vulnerability with the reader, a moral
and spiritual obligation follows. For him, writing is his
prayer. The act of prayer for Lopez is not religious but rather
a manner in which "to formalize the relationship between
yourself and a spiritual entity." Through his writing, Lopez
labors to "be aware of the spiritual dimension in people and
place and to evoke them as a reminder that this dimension is
present." His fiction reflects a technique of employing figura-
tive devices to approximate the inexplicable as explained in
The Jesuits by J.C.H. Aveling, whereby a "spiritual teaching in
words…tends to use deliberately startling flights of imagination and imagery to move and to convey the ultimately mysterious and incomprehensible."

Lopez's spirituality is nondenominational. His stories are
informed by an immersion in both Western and Eastern
philosophies, especially those of aboriginal peoples.
Although grounded in the fundamental rubrics of a devout
Roman Catholic upbringing that extended into college,
Lopez determined early on to consider "these other epistemologies" which he believed were "as rigorous and valid as
the ones [he] learned." Narrators in the role of *companion*,
rather than that of authority, wear many masks throughout
his short stories. His stories reveal an abiding desire to serve
and to provide for both human and nonhuman realms. To
this end, he humbly views himself as "just another guy
working in the garden" as a way of "trying to keep something alive in myself and in the world."

Understandably, a common misconception about Lopez is

that he is singularly a writer of natural history, otherwise known as the literature of place. Indeed, Lopez's roots do spring from an American literary tradition of inventory and social scrutiny that produced "Walden" and "On the Duty of Civil Disobedience" by Henry David Thoreau. He is often touted "as one of America's premier nature writers."

Lopez's worldwide reputation was established in the late 1970s and 1980s through writing natural history. *Of Wolves and Men* earned him the John Burroughs Medal for distinguished natural history writing, the Christopher Medal for humanitarian writing and the Pacific Northwest Booksellers' award for excellence in nonfiction in 1979. A National Book Award nomination followed in 1980. In 1986, he was the recipient of the National Book Award in nonfiction for *Arctic Dreams: Imagination and Desire in a Northern Landscape.* He received the *Los Angeles Times* book award nomination, the American Library Association Notable Book Citation, *The New York Times Book Review's* "Best Books" listing, and the American Library Association "Best Books for Young Adults" Citation for *Arctic Dreams.* Also, in 1986, Lopez received an award in literature for "body of work," from the American Academy and Institute of Arts and Letters. In 1987, he received the Francis Fuller Victor Award in nonfiction from the Oregon Institute of Literary Arts for *Arctic Dreams* and was awarded a John Simon Guggenheim Foundation fellowship. Grants from the National Science Foundation enabled him to participate in the Artists and Writers in Antarctica Program in 1987, 1988, 1991 and 1992.

Lopez is viewed as a champion of environmental issues, is perceived as one of the heirs to the legacy of Thoreau and Emerson and enjoys favorable comparisons to "such distinguished naturalists/authors as Edward Hoagland, Peter Matthiessen, Edward Abbey, Sally Carrighar, and Loren Eiseley." He received the John Hay Medal in 2001 and, like the medal's namesake, ardently believes our interaction with the planet's natural resources must transcend exploitation if we are to endure as a species. Lopez is quoted widely and is invited to participate in environmental dialogues throughout the world. The Explorers Club elected him a Fellow in 2002. On any number of environmental issues, his endorsement is sought due to the unwavering clarity of his vision, an altruistic nature and charismatic sincerity. He is regularly featured in books or articles about nature writers and writes forewords/ introductions and edits books with naturalistic overtures. A few recent titles include *The Land's Wild Music* (Trinity University 2005); *The Modern West: American Landscapes 1890-1950* (Yale University 2006); and *Home Ground: Language for an American Landscape* (Trinity University 2006).

Paradoxically, Lopez does not see himself "any more a nature writer than Steinbeck was." Although his fictive metaphors often highlight nature the subject is community, he claims. His writings have taproots in the landscape-evoking works of writers like Herman Melville and Willa Cather. Two writers specifically, Wallace Stegner and Wendell Berry, "taught me how to behave as a writer," claims Lopez. But, like them, the subject matter of his nonfiction is metaphorical, nonthreatening and unconsciously enlightening in the cryptic but classical fashion of fairy tales, fables, allegories and parables. More-over, Lopez does not conclude an inquiry into the physical world with either a naturalist's or biologist's formal training, although he acknowledges their inventories as invaluable. What is crucial to him is a gestalt of the ecological relationships in a locale, including human activity, that promotes social cohesiveness. Devotion to landscape and language drew him initially to natural history, a genre that historically never strays from seeking life-sustaining patterns. Concepts of community infuse all his writings. For Lopez, stories in particular are "the only safe containers for what consciousness" might be attained or intuited

about the human condition. When opting for a literary catego-
ry for Lopez, it might be useful to recall a line from the short
story, "Desert Notes": "You will think you have hold of the
idea when you only have hold of its clothing."

His body of literature recognizes neither genre boundaries
nor confining philosophical categories. Self-described as "a
writer who travels," Lopez shuns labels. Referring to his writing as chiseled or jewel-like is acceptable, but call him a prose
poet and he bristles at the notion that density of language is
the sole province of any genre. He moves as seamlessly among
writing disciplines as he does through landscapes in local and
distant indigenous cultures. Among earlier awards, the short
story "Benjamin Claire, North Dakota Tradesman, Writes to
the President of the United States" received a Pushcart Prize
in 1993. The audio edition of *About This Life,* which Lopez
recorded, "was one of three finalists for an Audi Award for
Best Abridged Nonfiction recording" in 1998. His childhood
memoir, "A Scary Abundance of Water," was nominated for a
Pulitzer Prize in 2002. *Resistance* won the H.L. Davis Award
for Short Fiction in 2005. In recognition of his literary contributions, on January 26, 2007, Notre Dame bestowed the
Rev. Robert J. Griffin Award on Lopez. His fiction and nonfiction are widely anthologized and have been translated into
languages that include Chinese, Dutch, Finnish, French,
German, Italian, Japanese, Norwegian, Portuguese, Russian,
Spanish and Swedish.

Throughout the gestation of his writing career, Lopez's
diversity and range in writing genres has resulted in wide-
spread appeal. First published in 1975, "My Horse" was
reprinted nearly two dozen times in high school textbooks.
Just as the timeless voice in *Of Wolves and Men* pleads for tolerance, so do the sagas of the childlike but ageless protagonists
in *Crow and Weasel* remind people of all ages to revere companionship and community. When Vintage launched a writer-

ly series of twelve modern authors, *Vintage Lopez* (Vintage 2004) included exemplary selections from both his nonfiction and fiction styles. He publishes regularly in *Harper's, The Paris Review, Orion, The Georgia Review, Granta* and *National Geographic,* contributes widely to books edited by others, is currently a corresponding editor for *Manoa* and actively engages in collaborative projects with fellow artists. These have included working with the composer John Luther Adams and speaking at exhibitions which have presented the works of sculptor Michael Singer and that of photographer Robert Adams. He has also collaborated with Jim Leonard, Jr., the playwright; with Manfred Eicher, the producer of ECM Records; with Robin Eschner, a painter and wood block artist; with Tom Pohrt, an illustrator; with Richard Nelson, a writer; with Alan Magee, an artist; and with David Darling, a cellist, whose music inspired "Disturbing the Night," a short story by Lopez that reminds the reader of the redemptive power of forgiveness. Along these lines is an underlying theme of reconciliation, which is being anthologized in two volumes of *Manoa* that its editor, Frank Stewart, and Lopez are presently culling from earlier volumes. The first volume, *Maps of Reconciliation: Literature and the Ethical Imagination,* arrived in February 2008. With coeditor Debra Gwartney, Lopez drew on the talents of forty-five writers, including poets, for *Home Ground.* Scheduled for 2010, at the San Francisco Museum of Modern Art, is an exhibit of landscape photographs that will include *Home Ground* entries.

In addition to numerous honors, grants and awards, in Lopez's literary wake are invitations as guest speaker, writer-in-residence and scholar. In 1985, he became an associate at the Gannett Foundation Media Center at Columbia University in New York City; a Distinguished Visiting Writer at Eastern Washington University in Cheney, Washington; and the Ida Beam Visiting Professor at the University of Iowa, in Iowa

City. In 1986, he was the Distinguished Visiting Naturalist at Carleton College in Northfield, Minnesota. He was a delegate, in 1988, at the Sino-American Writers Conference in China. Whittier College bestowed an honorary L.H.D. on him in 1988. In 1989, he was the W. Harold and Martha Welch Visiting Professor of American Studies at the University of Notre Dame in Notre Dame, Indiana. In 1994, he was invited to deliver an invocation for the inauguration of Governor Barbara Roberts, Oregon's first female governor. Since 2001, he has been catalystic at Texas Tech University in establishing social justice programs. He and Edward O. Wilson, preeminent Harvard entomologist and Pulitzer Prize winning author— whose book length epistle, *The Creation: An Appeal to Save Life on Earth,* successfully wooed evangelicals to partner with scientists so as to protect the planet's complex and yet unfathomed biodiversity—designed an undergraduate major in Natural History & the Humanities at TTU. In 2003, Lopez became their Visiting Distinguished Scholar. In May 2006, he provided the ending presentation, "Eden is a Conversation," at the Quest for Global Healing in Ubud, Bali, Indonesia. In March 2007, Lopez was one of the honorees who spoke at the annual dinner of The Explorers Club. Each year he travels extensively around the country so as to provide presentations at numerous venues. These include civic centers, college campuses and bookstores, with their times/places faithfully updated on his website at www.barrylopez.com.

Lopez's self-described "Grail Quest" is "to underscore the need to share." His commitment to fostering the well-being of local and global communities is evident throughout his body of literature and his lifestyle. He maintains that the calamities of our age have solutions in the creative "genius of community." At times, his private actions appear as manifestations of his own fictive characters who have reconciled with soul-shaking terrors to lead worthy lives. He often trades large blocks of time—essential, he wistfully acknowledges, to establishing writing rhythms—in pursuit of more direct community-building activities: providing a voice for worthy causes, tutoring students/younger writers, public speaking/facilitating and artistic collaboration. Without fanfare, his actions embody ideals expressed in *The Rediscovery of North America.* Nowhere is this more evident than through his behind-the-scenes' initiatives at Texas Tech University. These encompass complex social and cultural issues involving reconciliation between the university and the Comanche Nation. They also include curriculum development in respect to enlightened concepts of ethics involving Southwestern cultural geography and water conservation. Lopez shuns the spotlight and prefers to be another thread "in the fabric of our own diverse communities." For some readers, his altruism will fuel society's insatiable need for parody and caricature. The rest of us will be reminded, "The way we take care of ourselves is by taking care of each other."

Nowadays, age has forced Lopez to hesitate in embarking on similar rugged wilderness adventures of his youth which were physically grueling and posed significant risk. Neither is he inclined to generate writing that inadvertently betrays the numinous of a place, an environy that occurred when tourists assailed the Arctic upon the publication of *Arctic Dreams* and when the ground glyph that prompted "The Stone Horse" was vandalized.

Lopez is anything but world-weary, though. Other writing and travel beckon. A McDowell Colony residency, in 2006, allowed him a clearer sense of the direction for *Horizons,* which has been an extensive work-in-progress for nearly a decade. Overlaps of culture and nature offer "an important arena for political writing." He longs to travel in Australia with the landscape painter John Wolseley, and he's "always wanted to do a story about fabric." Most telling, he and

Debra Gwartney—long-time domestic partners—married on December 15, 2007.

The short stories of Barry Lopez are anchored in a classical heritage in which fiction delves into the Great Mystery of Being. For him, these "blueprints for the imagination" are simply the most efficient vehicle for reminding himself and his readers of what community-sustaining patterns might be intuited "in the world of comparative ways of knowing."

> *One of the marvelous things about story, about what story does, is that it creates both a surface reality and a reality in parallel, which allows you to appreciate something both directly and indirectly, some aspect of life obliquely. Story has a way of disarming or dismantling the flow of time by its use of tense; it creates an environment where the mind can rest; it can move about and come to feel coherent or healed.*

The Short Story Books

Desert Notes: Reflections in the Eye of a Raven (1976) is the first book of twelve short stories in a trilogy that includes *River Notes: The Dance of Herons* and *Field Notes: The Grace Note of the Canyon Wren*. *Desert Notes* was written when Lopez was probably twenty-four, affectionately called by him a young man's invention for its unselfconscious prose and naiveté and was never intended by him for publication. On the same day Jim Andrews received the manuscript for *Desert Notes,* he enthusiastically telephoned Lopez to advise him that this should be his first book. "This is the way you should be introduced as a writer." Photographs by the author inform this book. On the dustjacket, the golden glow of a rocking chair setting on a cracked desert floor, with distant mountains ascending into a blue sky, suggests the pinstripe between fact and fiction that is a signature of his stories.

Throughout many of his stories are thinly guised sidebars of a Roman Catholic, Jesuit upbringing. Lopez's propensity for the monastic life—one of spiritual kinship with the land; satisfying, physical labor; and minimal technological intrusion—may spring from a Desert Father tradition (i.e., St. Anthony, St. Paul and St. Jerome). Also known as anchorites, these spiritual hermits shun civilization's turmoil and temptations. It is a lifestyle that Lopez wrangled with as a young man, when he considered entering a Trappist monastery in Kentucky. Central to several short stories in this book are circumstances in which his protagonists almost appear to favor a monastic or Desert Father existence. This is in contrast to the "Teal Creek" protagonist in *Field Notes,* who is conflicted by a hermit's beatific isolation but resurfaces with the "The Construction of the Rachel" protagonist in *Light Action in the Caribbean,* who retreats to a monastic life upon learning of his wife's infidelity. In each story their personae provide or suggest instructions reminiscent of *The Spiritual Exercises of Saint Ignatius,* written by the sixteenth-century founder of the Jesuits, St. Ignatius of Loyola.

Learning to avoid what is unnecessary is an oft-repeated refrain. "Introduction" instructs the reader to abandon his techno-umbilical cord "through a series of strippings." The narrator drives onto the desert floor somewhere in the American West and then proceeds with a succession of peregrinations that allow his van to inch along unattended in low gear while he casually climbs in and out its doors, then bikes in the opposite direction and returns to jog alongside. "Desert Notes" alerts the reader "that we must get all these things about time and place straight." To do this requires attentiveness, patience and a willingness to "take things down to the core."

Physical deprivation, solitude and a meditative bearing provide for spiritual awareness. In "The Hot Spring," the narrator travels alone on an exhaustive journey past "a golden eagle sitting on a fence post." This is significant in that the Plains Indians believe the feathers of a golden eagle provide access to the spirits, much as the story's unnamed persona is "careful with the silence" in an attempt to connect with his spiritual self. Naked, he enters the hot springs and appears to undergo baptism/rebirth. Upon leaving "the sulphurous fumes rising up from the green reeds," he feels reborn and senses "the pressure of his parting the air." The image of a Desert Father is complete when he drinks water and eats cereal from an earthen bowl.

"Directions" is the last story in this book and may be the most prescient of all. It echoes the Percival quest, requiring personal sacrifice and courage to provide light in a world of darkness. Also known as the Perfect Fool for his innocence, Percival was one of King Arthur's knights whose earthly sloggings while in pursuit of the Holy Grail characterize the quest motif. As with many of Lopez's questers, narrators encounter wilderness hermits who test their worthiness. So it happens that man-made maps are to be avoided in favor of a mythic journey helper who could be an older version of the protagonist the reader meets in "Introduction" and resurfaces ultimately in *Light Action in the Caribbean* as Corlis Benefideo in "The Mappist." In "Directions," the narrator provides the usual set of intricate instructions which include patience, sincerity of purpose and an opportunity to "never again hear a map so well spoken" as from an unlikely holy man named Leon. Leon has been to the "famous desert" that the narrator alludes to. What makes this desert attractive is its potential for unveiling a deep mystery that will transform one's personal chaos into a serene, cosmic paradigm.

Each book in the trilogy has a subtitle which suggests a

totemic connection to the landscape. All are birds, but why? And why the raven, the largest and most adaptive, all-black passerine bird in the Northern Hemisphere? Lopez had raised tumbler pigeons in his youth in California and, to this day, remains spellbound by the invisible axis on which those winged creatures plunge earthwards. He had even majored briefly in aeronautical engineering as an undergraduate at Notre Dame.

The raven enjoys occult status in many cultures. Legend has the raven feeding St. Paul the Hermit and St. Anthony in the desert. A black raven and a white raven were referred to as mind and memory by the Norse god, Odin. A superstition has England preserved as long as there are ravens in the Tower of London. The raven luxuriates in Trickster myths through-out the Northern Hemisphere, whereby voracious appetites and passions propel him into a medley of raucous escapades. Lopez might well have been drawn to Raven as Trickster through his Native American folklore studies. In his poem entitled "Ravens," the persona speaks of how he and another, who is apparently adept in woods' craft, are "fooled by ravens. Even you" as both men tentatively approach what they believe to be a mountain lion kill.

Lopez assigns the bird a prophetic role in his short story called "The Raven," whereby the bird assumes the role of seer in the creature kingdom. The reader is petitioned to under-stand the raven through the disappearance of crows in the desert. The solitary raven is metaphorically contrasted to the overpopulating, flock-fouling crow. Its loathsome habit of killing owls for sport-and-spite provides an allegory for Western man's senseless depredations. The crow's unwilling-ness to prosper from the raven's sage counsel explains its ulti-mate absence from the desert. This story could very well be Lopez's signature piece in the book. The terms for survival in any particular landscape require an ability like the raven's, "to grasp and hold fast, not to puncture."

The consequences of estrangement with the land are another recurring motif. "Coyote and Rattlesnake" is a fable that likely evolved during the period in which Lopez was deeply involved with Northern American folklore. Its plot presages the end of Shisa, or Man, who is noisy "like a boulder fallen off a mountain" that comes to a stop. Coyote commiserates with Rattlesnake over his disgust with Shisa who was originally "trapped inside the flowers before dawn." Shisa's mindlessness toward other living creatures has caused great misery. Shisa takes without giving back and conducts himself without acknowledging "something could not come from nothing." It is noteworthy that even Coyote receives instructions regarding patience, attentiveness and the need for purification rites so as to be worthy of an audience with a divine presence.

The rich irony of "The School" is self-evident. It is one of few stories with first and last names and a traditional storyline. The plot centers around an abandoned school house, which was built midway between a town and a cinnabar mine, over thirty miles away, that eventually gave out. The fictional perspective flows from an older graduate who comes every few years to "try and clean it out, burn up the garbage." Bullet holes and other predictable forms of vandalism intermingle with tender accounts regarding classmates and maple floorboards brought "two hundred miles on the train." The tone is melancholic and foreshadows the fate of a civilization that would be the master of the land rather than its companion.

Mankind's destructive acts which result when he loots the natural resources of a watershed is pervasive throughout Lopez's work. This righteous anger reaches a crescendo in his treatise, *The Rediscovery of North America* (1991), which was originally presented as the first Thomas D. Clark Lecture at the University of Kentucky in 1990. Lopez used that opportunity to challenge the listener/reader to "establish some sense of reciprocity with the Earth, some sense of what is owed back and forth."

"The Blue Mound People" is paradoxical. It contradicts the notion that an abiding sense of the land is a guarantee for eternal prosperity. In this story a cave-dwelling, meditative people, who appeared to have maintained an equitable relationship with the desert they inhabited, inexplicably "all died within the period of a year." At the center of their lives was "a series of blue earth mounds." Each mound contained "a hard, white stone" that suggested a metaphysical bond. The narrator provides convincing scientific-like data to concoct a tone of credibility. Yet, the blue-gray skinned, white-haired and gray-eyed people who lived in caves that "have been shifting a little to the north each year" are cloaked in a storytelling mirage. The reader must ponder the infinite, varying subtleties required "to become the companion of a place." Also in question is whether human habitation is warranted in biologically fragile landscapes or where human survival is dependent on tenuous conditions.

Desert Notes is a significant literary accomplishment for a young writer whose primary motive was "an impulse to write out the way I look at things." It is a measure of what can occur when "you wait for yourself," as the narrator advises in "Conversation." In this story, an interior dialogue establishes philosophical anchor points similar to the web strands of a spider so "sunlight will bounce when it hits." In a classic Trickster maneuver, the value of metaphor is artfully dismissed by the narrator when it is actually an axis on which many of Lopez's themes spin. This slender volume, described as having "jewel-like prose" provides the reader with a poignant glimpse of issues and themes dear to Lopez. *Desert Notes* has been praised as "one of the most sensitive and lyrical evocations of nature since Annie Dillard's *Pilgrim At Tinker Creek.*" Edward Abbey described the book as going "straight

THE SHORT STORY BOOKS OF BARRY LOPEZ |

to the heart of the peculiar sensations, both physical and mental, known to all who have allowed themselves open communion with the land."

Surrealism, magical realism and pantheism have been literary scaffoldings assigned to Lopez's work but which he dismisses as missing the mark. More likely candidates are the paradoxical Trickster figure, with Herman Melville as his moral and literary linchpin, and a profound love for desert-like landscapes which allow "a context in which to sort out abstract ideas" which Lopez compares to trace elements of zinc that are essential to the health of humans.

River Notes: The Dance of Herons (1979), with twelve short stories, is the second book in this trilogy. There were photographs by Lopez intended for these stories, as well, but the only one included is on the dustjacket of the hardcover edition. It is of a pair of colorful Western Sioux moccasins located on a boulder either in or near a fast moving river. This book was published a year after *Giving Birth to Thunder, Sleeping with His Daughter* (1978). Also published in that year was *Of Wolves and Men* (1978), an environmental blockbuster for which Lopez received worldwide recognition and which has become a rallying cry for social issues of intolerance, prejudice and stereotyping.

The stories in *River Notes* examine cyclic events and geographic features that might occur along any wilderness river, but which ultimately nest in the human psyche. In cascading prose, the reader tumbles through log jams, rapids and waterfalls, moves among the shallows and experiences the sensation of drought. By the time these stories were written, Lopez had lived near the McKenzie River in Western Oregon for nearly a decade. Its influence on his storyweaving was demonstrated while we were driving across a bridge over the McKenzie. Lopez stated how the bridge had been the basis for a "logging bridge" in "The Log Jam."

The Victorian "I" still infuses these stories, along with "a landscape of facts so convincing it gains the authority of non-fiction." Human death occurs in these pages, but it is a hallmark of Lopez's first four books that people in his stories do not harm one another. They may expire as a result of accident, ignorance or loss of grace but never by malevolence. Some stories even have names for their characters, although the reader is more likely to encounter place names for geographic formations.

An undercurrent of anguish pervades the pages of *River Notes* and shakes the narrators to their spiritual core. Lopez noted, "*Desert Notes* is playful, but there's no playfulness in *River Notes.*" "Introduction" begins this book with "a sound that would make you cry at the thought of what had slipped through your fingers." The story opens with the narrator at a crossroads in a quest that is mysteriously quixotic. He suffers from self-delusion, is spiritually exhausted and questions his worthiness, as did Percival. The headwaters, so to speak, for this book was personal grief. Many reviewers were understandably enthralled by its "rhythmical, muscular, poetic writing" style. But it took a question-and-answer period, after a reading of his work, for Lopez to reveal the alluvia for his narrators' torment. A student at Carleton College commented to Lopez that the tone of the book signaled a tragic personal loss by its author. Those in the audience who thought the remark impertinent were silenced when Lopez quietly acknowledged that the stories were informed by the dying of his mother. In this short story, the narrator's mother also dies, but the fictional son did not believe his grief pure in that he coveted "her small teakwood trunk with the beautiful brass fittings and its silver padlock."

In classic Lopezean fashion, however, narrators consumed by guilt, malaise or despair overcome their emotional paralysis by undergoing a spiritual rejuvenation which is triggered by a synergy of self-examination, cleansing rituals and wilderness pilgrimages. These provide for a "loss of guile," as angst is quelled, "when your fingers brush the soft skin of a deer-head orchid and you see sun-drenched bears stretching in an open field."

"The Search for the Heron" is essentially a quest for a spiritual guide. It is a fitting title piece, and the heron is an apt emblem to represent the primal pain one might associate with the loss of either one's mother or other spiritual provider. Heron is a word distantly related to *krizein*, a Greek word which means "to cry out or shriek," not unlike the narrators whose keening is heard throughout this book. Likewise, the heron is also considered a phoenix-like bird, whose rebirth is analogous and essential to that of the narrator's. In this story, the protagonist follows the heron in a belief that he can "expect the wisdom of the desert out of [it]."

In Lopez's animistic world, everything dreams, including boulders and herons. Dreaming is associated with a vision quest and plays a prominent role in the story. The narrator not only becomes unnerved upon learning the dreams of the heron but also becomes less frenzied by discovering the source of its pain. There is a chanticler-styled allusion when the heron experiences the loss of his daughter by not listening to his own dream. In supplication, the narrator purges himself by taking "bits of bone from fish [it] had eaten" and piercing his fingers.

As with other stories, like "Perimeter" in *Desert Notes,* quaternity or the element of fourness arises often enough to suggest more than randomness. In an earlier story the reference included the cardinal directions, whereas in this story there is a hint of the divine associated with the Hermetic philosophy of the Middle Ages. The narrator has "a great dream" upon observing the edge-shadows of a fire for four nights. In it the heron releases a snake that sought to harm it, whereupon the narrator learns to dispel fear—that breeder of misunderstanding and reckless violence—and to replace it with compassion. Awakening, both in body and through heightened consciousness, "an unpronounceable forgiveness" overwhelms the narrator. He baptizes himself in the winter river and notices the heron "begin to appear at a downriver bend." This suggests future philosophical log jams for which the heron healer can provide further relief.

"The Log Jam" and "The Rapids" are more traditional in scope, with names, dates and action-packed storylines. Both begin with the anguish of human death and end in quiet refrain regarding the private emotional channels individuals must navigate so as to reconcile their grief. Within the first story, the narrator tracks the history of a log jam from 1946 to 1973. The story reflects on the saga of human interaction with a landscape not unlike more classical human domiciles, which were built one atop the other.

Using lyrical imagery in "The Log Jam," the author describes how "a big tree barberchairing" crushes a logger. His distraught son dumps its trunk into the river, where it washes up against an island downstream. In 1951, a non-swimming father miraculously saves his nonswimming son from drowning. The maple limb he tosses aside floats downstream to the log jam. In 1954, a violent windstorm lasting only minutes knocks trees into the river. They, in turn, become part of the history of the river by joining the log jam. A woman spreads petals from twenty years' worth of anniversaries and friendships into the river. They become part of the log jam in 1957. Alder branches, in 1964, sweep down to the log jam. They have been dislodged by a boy trying to coax beaver out of their den so he can shoot them, to no avail. The crown of a fir tree, over 400 years old, falls into the river and also becomes part of the log jam. Finally, a pair of osprey build a nest and "lived as well as could be expected in that country."

"The Rapids" puts the question "why" to rest. A reporter's insensitive inquiries following a river drowning extract hostility from locals. The reader will feel hurled through a chute by the speed of the dialogue in the story and the emotional turbulence of unanswerable questions. It is only through an older man's reconciliation with his past, when his wife drowned while he was able to save himself, that anger and blame are suspended. The news scoop sought by the reporter is best expressed by the old man, whose remarks reveal a macabre twist of what it ultimately means to realize a landscape's companionship—namely, the locality where loved ones perish. He refuses to move away from the site of personal tragedy, since "it's easiest to live where you have an understanding."

In "The Bend," the protagonist suffers from deep, chronic depression which incapacitates him. He seeks meaning from the river, like the pursuer of the heron, but goes about it in a way that only adds to his misery. Here, Lopez may be speaking indirectly about Western man's fatal flaw of relying exclusively on the quantifying aspects of technology to gauge an object's worth. The protagonist hires a medley of scientists, including hydrologists and surveyors, so as to calculate "an elegant series of equations" to a bend in the river. The bend is symbolic in that the protagonist is at a philosophical "bend" himself. It is not until the calculations with all their attendant notes are piled into a corner that the protagonist begins to recover from his malady. The notes morph into river sounds, moss grows on them and they resemble gray boulders. Bears bring him to the river where he begins "to feel, raccoonlike, with the tips" of his fingers. Like the persona in Walt Whitman's "When I Heard the Learn'd Astronomer," who shuns the lecture hall and "look[s] up in perfect silence at the stars," the narrator acknowledges how companionship, not authority, has "dismantled my loneliness."

"Drought" is heartwrenching. The reader is reminded that, like leaves falling into the river, he is "only commentary on the river's endless reading of the surface of the earth over which it flows." The river is eternal, but human beings are not. When the protagonist uses the analogy of returning "as one visits those dying helplessly in a hospital room," the reader is reminded of the author's own dying mother. The protagonist fasts, abstains and prays in suppliant gestures that would bestow grace on the dying river. As the river drops, a Kiplingesque "peace rock" emerges in the form of pools from which deer and coyote sip. Irrationally, the protagonist nearly yields to "a loss of conviction, to rage, to hurling what beliefs [he] had... into the bushes." What brings him back from the abyss is his capacity to set aside his own sense of loss in order to rescue a hapless fish. This selfless act moves Blue Heron to teach him a dance that brings not just water but spiritual nourishment. Through personal sacrifice, the protagonist "remembers how to live." This is enough to rejuvenate the river. Painfully, but with profound compassion, the narrator acknowledges reconciliation with the inevitable death awaiting human beings. "Everyone has to learn how to die, that song, that dance, alone and in time." Within simple but heartfelt agreements and understandings, the river will always rise. The narrator delves his hands into the rising river, realizing it is the cord that binds "the earth together in one piece."

What *Desert Notes* intones, *River Notes* affirms. Lopez coaxes the "wisdom of the desert" from these stories. Desert themes re-emerge in primeval splendor along a river that is "an energized, original metaphor of life." Other themes surface that become more fully realized in Lopez's later short story books, most notably "of things so beautiful they made you afraid." The lyrical qualities of language and imagery move these short stories into the realm of parable. It is the work of a writer locating his own particular voice. The literary seams are less apparent in this second book. Imagination reigns without the intrusions of "isms," i.e., magical realism. Upon the publication of *River Notes,* critics hailed Lopez as a "deft stylist." Edward Abbey described him as "an artist in language." Diane Wakoski declared that "his work had the fascination of document."

Winter Count (1981) received the Distinguished Recognition Award from the Friends of American Writers in 1982. It is Lopez's third book and contains nine short stories, but does not complete the set. When he signed a contract in 1974 for the trilogy that begins with *Desert Notes,* he had some idea of what *River Notes* would be, but no clear ideas about the third book. "Winter count" alludes to the custom by America's Northern Plains' peoples of recording significant events "pictographically on a buffalo robe or spoken aloud." In similar fashion, Lopez skillfully paints these stories in hues that bear witness to drama and mystery. There is no subtitle nor introduction which characterized the first two books. Neither is there a centering, totemic bird figure although, in "Winter Herons," nearly twenty great blue herons dreamily descend "as if on a prairie" amidst a snowfall in the concrete canyons of New York City.

Nor are there photographs. Lopez put down the camera for good in 1981, having concluded that its use precluded other observations essential to a writer. Provocative illustrations by Ted Lewin appear on the dustjacket and precede each of nine stories. Their presence heralds Lopez's collaboration with fellow artists. Later, this will result in exquisitely illustrated, limited editions of his short stories and in his best-selling children's book, *Crow and Weasel* (1990), which received the Parents' Choice Award in 1990. Other awards include the Lannan Foundation Award in nonfiction (1990), for body-of-work; the Governor's Award for Arts (1990); and the Best Geographic Educational Article, National Council for Geographic

Education (1990) for "The American Geographies."

Quotations preceding this short story book remind the reader of two Lopezean provisos: the values of listening and of the imagination. What strikes the reader about this book is Lopez's capacity to elicit beauty and life-affirmation through plots in which fictive characters must often endure daunting anguish. He achieves this, in part, through quest motifs in which the stories' protagonists seek "proof against some undefined but irrefutable darkness in the world." In each story but one, the narrators bring with them a background of exotic travel, as does Lopez. In accordance with the pattern of quests, it is significant that the narrators travel in unfamiliar landscapes and are introduced to the reader at life-defining "bends" or moments. No longer are his characters shrouded in anonymity. Not only do they have names, but their biographical circumstances are meticulously detailed. What is distinctive about these stories is the added dimension of humanity that inculcates Lopez's plots/characters and may be a benchmark by which to gauge his subsequent writings in fiction *and* nonfiction. Conflicts in *Winter Count* involve deeply private but universal struggles characteristic of the human condition. As evocative as the language was in his earlier short stories, a muscled suppleness emerges in this book. Time no longer feels suspended. There is a seamless quality in delivery, and internal dialogues verify a peopled world.

Scant else appears to carry denser moral weight for Lopez than the responsibility to "honor the unspoken request of our companions to speak the truth." In "Restoration," a narrator driving through North Dakota in 1974 encounters an itinerant bookbinder engaged in the "accurate and sympathetic restoration" of several hundred leather-bound volumes which date back to the sixteenth century. The books once belonged to a Frenchman from the late 1800s, whose ancestors had settled that region.

As is so beguiling with Lopez, there is often a story within the story. The reader might initially believe that the story revolves around the artistic integrity of an elderly gentleman as he first "beveled a frayed corner clean and then anchored a new piece of book board to it with tiny steel pins, like a bone fracture." Later on he disclaims shellacs in favor of "egg whites and vinegar." The ruse is complete when the bookwright leaves the usual written evidence of repair inside a restored volume, so as not to appear deceptive. The "story" may not be about book restoration.

With vintage Lopezean understatement, "Restoration" fuses a technique of suggestion with intoxicating lyrical imagery to present an abstract concept that is heretical to Western mindsets. More to a viable point of the story, elaborately expressed in *Of Wolves and Men* and prophetic to Lopez's essay of 1990, *The Rediscovery of North America,* is the Frenchman's obsession with establishing "a *new* understanding, rooted in North America and representing a radically different view of the place of animals in human ideas." This viewpoint dismisses the European bias that labels animals as soul-less creatures, recognizes their impact on Native American philosophies and acknowledges their birthright as "owners of the landscape." Lopez's capacity to meld ideas into story is a distinguishing trait. What John Day champions through *In Defense of Nature* and what Roderick Nash explains in *Wilderness and the American Mind,* Lopez accomplishes with story.

The title piece, "Winter Count 1973: Geese, They Flew Over in a Storm," directly addresses the role of the storyteller and indirectly questions attitudes of cultural superiority by experts who would discount "the individual view, the poetic view, which is as close to the truth as the consensus." The latter reflects an observation by Lopez in *Of Wolves and*

Men, whereby indigenous people regard each wolf as an individual with unique personality quirks while outsiders tend to generalize and stereotype.

In "Winter Count," an elderly anthropologist, whose field of inquiry has been the cultures of the Plains' peoples, reluctantly agrees to present a paper at a convention in New Orleans. Years of observing the cultural habits of indigenous North Americans openly influence his comportment, which is viewed as flawed by colleagues more concerned with their own professional canonization. In his hotel room, he hangs a medicine bundle, consisting of "a beaded bag of white elk hide with long fringe," from a tripod made of willow sticks. He prefers deep listening to authoritative proselytizing. He will "only tell the story as it was given" to him, without embellishment or self-aggrandizement. Insights into the cultures he's dedicated his career to have humbled him and have engendered in him a sense of appreciative humility toward their cultures.

Like the protagonists in earlier stories who have "thrown away everything that is no good," this narrator agonizes over the noxious violation of trust that occurs in any position paper "proving you are right." Once again the reader is gently urged to consider that stories and compassion are "all that is holding us together." The story concludes with a haiku-like montage of "barking-dog sounds of geese, running like horses before a prairie thunderstorm."

What transpires when even enlightened Western minds wrangle with the Trickster figure is the basis for "The Location of the River." Some time before 1963, the narrator comes into possession of tattered documents compiled by Benjamin Foster, a cultural historian who began living among the North American Plains' peoples nearly a hundred-and-fifty years earlier. Foster lives and travels with the Pawnee, the Arikara, the Arapaho, the Oglala Sioux and others over a span of three decades, as he attempts to record their beliefs before "they fell victim to whites or to the panic of their own spiritual leaders."

A chance remark by a Pawnee about the Niobrara River disappearing altogether from "a sort of willful irritation" toward the white man's take-for-granted attitude impels Foster on a fruitless quest. His traditional methods of inquiry release an internal cultural maelstrom as he pursues an event incomprehensible to Western dogma and the limitations of scientific inquiry. Only when Foster succumbs to *wakan*, the gift of preternatural powers, does the incredible event of the river unfurl "in the shapes of the towering cumulus clouds that moved over the country." This episode erodes Foster's faith in his ability to accurately record the beliefs of the peoples of the Great Basin. Self-doubt capitulates to madness when "ritual cleansing and dreaming" fail to absolve an even earlier accusation. A Piegan, with the suspiciously familiar Trickster moniker of Coyote-in-the-Camp, tells Foster that he is "learning everything wrong." When the narrator attempts to clarify Foster's observations by visiting the Niobrara, he is inexplicably waylaid by flood waters that chase him from that country for good.

Four stories address the malaise triggered by the death of a parent, by the human condition of separateness and by *sharawadji*, a graceful disorder. In "The Orrery," a young man encounters a Desert Father when he embarks on a pilgrimage to the Arizona desert in a quest to locate a rare cactus named after his deceased father. The older man's intimacy with the desert is apparent when he casually refers to the cactus in question as being useful to treat depression. He shows the narrator an orrery, which is an apparatus that depicts the relationship of the planets in our solar system. When he purposefully sweeps the desert floor with a broom in what can only be described as "an impossible task," similar to that of prayer, the narrator suspends judgment. The old man doesn't suffer from dementia, but is actually seeking perfectly proportioned stones to represent celestial bodies in the galaxy. Later that evening, as celestial winds lift the stones and hold them in the night sky, the young man learns "there is probably nothing that cannot be retrieved" through faith and belief in one's task.

In "The Tapestry," a grieving son travels to Spain to attend to his deceased father's affairs. While there, a journey helper in the guise of a curator at the Prado Museum introduces the young man to a tapestry his grandfather had once owned. Within beautifully depicted "scenes of rustic and courtly life" can be sensed a foreboding "of some catastrophe or other" that could represent the inevitable abyss awaiting all life-forms. Rather than rage in indignation or cower in trepidation, the characters within the tapestry follow St. Ignatio's advice when facing impending destruction—to "go on doing whatever you are doing." Upon grasping the disingenuous message in the tapestry, the narrator sheds emotional turmoil as he is "rid of a daunting exhortation to examine life."

A muse-like creature appears for the narrator in "The Woman Who Had Shells." She evinces the sublime. The narrator first observes a woman engaged in "cranelike movements," as she cups shells to her cheek along a beach on Sanibel, an island off the west coast of Florida. He is enthralled by her expression "seen before only in the face of a friend who paints, when he has finished, when the mystery is established and accepted without explanation."

The following year in late winter, he chances upon her as she sits in a restaurant in New York City. Their spirited conversation brings them to her apartment. Their actions are sensual but not sexual and so follows the story's imagery and rhythm. Colors of "mikado yellow, cerulean blue and crimson flush" intermingle with fluted shells "delicately tinged" or with "patterns like African fabric and inscriptions of

Chinese characters." Through this spiritually generative rendezvous, the narrator "imagined it was possible to let go of a fundamental anguish."

One of few short stories told in the third person is "The Lover of Words." The plot describes the spiritual disintegration of a gardener of Mexican descent, once he stumbles over a philosophical stone. He lives in the "barrio of East Los Angeles" and makes his living in Beverly Hills. Gifted with his hands and not crushed by the racism around him, he also "understood how words healed." Internal conflicts "between ideas and work" pervade his thoughts. He becomes despondent. A reckless reaching within the ideas-of-ideas triggers a spiritual maelstorm. He becomes dissatisfied with his passions. Intuitive talents are initially questioned and then become inaccessible. Cultural disparities preoccupy him and hasten a downward spiral of self-doubt. A discovery of the word *ahimsa*, the right of living things to be respected, further causes him to question the moral issue of summarily selecting what will flourish and what will perish in those landscapes he cultivates. There is no outward explanation for his malaise, only the implication that its ominous seeds lie dormant in our genetic codes.

Eventually, the gardener regains a sense of spiritual balance upon appreciating "the sight of his hard, blunt thumbs against the white pages of a book" and thinking "of the inscrutable life buried in a wheelbarrow full of bulbs." Like the protagonist in "The Bend," his recovery is dependent upon surrendering to that which nurtures life-sustaining energies in the world. This will not insulate him from "other bends in the river as dangerous farther on," but it will provide for atonement.

Equipped with a Trickster's toolbag of literary techniques accessed through years of researching for and writing nonfiction, Lopez concocts imaginative details that playfully befuddle and intoxicate. The stories in *Winter Count* are neither autobiographical nor historical, although they shimmer with ghost light from actual events and intersperse imaginary with real landscapes.

Like the young man in "The Tapestry," Lopez is "the product of a rigorous Jesuit education" and did visit Europe after graduation from high school. His fascination with cultural anthropology spawned an exhaustive inquiry into Native American cultures and resulted in his first book, a book of Trickster stories called *Giving Birth to Thunder, Sleeping with His Daughter* (1978). References to California emerge in autobiographical clips that could be lifted from *About This Life* (1998), a book of essays sown with personal detail. Lopez is as well traveled as any of his characters and can be perceived as exuding an "inpenetrable privacy." Although older than either protagonist in "The Orrery" or "The Tapestry," which were written after he lost a parent, Lopez was thirty-one when his beloved mother died. As evidenced by the overall tone of *River Notes* and by references in *About This Life,* he grieved deeply.

In *Winter Count,* Lopez's protagonists continue to grapple with issues of complacency, of isolation and of what Thoreau describes as "quiet desperation." So do many readers. Thankfully, a trademark of Lopez is to provide pathways for readers to follow his characters back from whatever abyss they encounter in their journeys. Reviewers lavished praise on *Winter Count.* William Kittredge described it as "radiant with possibilities which transcend the defeats we find for ourselves." Arturo Vivante claimed that "the reader has the feeling he has finally found a guide he can trust."

Field Notes: The Grace Note of the Canyon Wren (1994) received the Pacific Northwest Booksellers' award in fiction in 1995 and the Critics' Choice award in 1996. This book of twelve short stories completes the trilogy of *Desert Notes* and

River Notes. Originally, this book was to be called *Animal Notes,* but the impulse toward that book evolved into *Of Wolves and Men* (1978). Written over twenty years after *Desert Notes, Field Notes* celebrates Lopez's growth as a writer, his global travels and his worldwide reputation as an advocate of environmental issues. In recognition of his contributions, the University of Portland conferred an honorary L.H.D. on him in 1994.

Most notably, the stories are influenced by "25 years of apprenticeship to a non-Western point of view" and "hinge on questions of whether the narrator is hearing what the world is telling him." *Field Notes'* seamless style is more representative of *Winter Count,* "an indicator of where [he] wanted to go as a fiction writer." The stories were crafted in a seven-month period in 1992 and appear in the order they were written. Like all his "collections" of short stories, Lopez views *Field Notes* as a *book* and "not just arbitrary gatherings of stories." Whereas landscapes connect *Desert Notes* and *River Notes,* "*Winter Count, Field Notes* and *Light Action in the Caribbean* are thematically linked."

As with *Winter Count,* the protagonists in *Field Notes* participate fully in a peopled world. The stories are vintage Lopez. Universal themes of "human dignity and the nature of tolerance" percolate from within timeless plots in which subtlety, understatement and self-examination prevail. Their motifs explore the inherent terrors that result from human consciousness and shattered complacency, the timely appearance of journey helpers in the guise of Desert Fathers and the ability of techno-man to significantly reconnect with the rhythms of the universe.

These stories' events unfold in small rural communities, cities, foreign lands and dreamscapes in modern or contemporary times. As is customary with Lopez's characters, they remain inquisitive, receptive to the sublime, formally educated or enlightened and are introduced to the reader as they engage in spiritual quests/odysseys, either by intent or serendipity. Unlike the earlier books, a female presence is salient. Visages of what might have been regarded as magical realism in the earlier books have yielded to quest visions that appear shamanistic in their origins and presentations. Like *Winter Count,* the characters' privacy is no longer a primary consideration. With the author's imagination and deft eye for detail, their backgrounds and mannerisms are meticulously portrayed in a highly provocative prose style. All stories but one in this book are anchored in landscapes vibrantly expressed and turn on the narrators' relationships to geographical references convincingly summoned.

Unlike the earlier books, neither photographs nor illustrations appear in these pages. On the hardcover dust jacket is a 1978 photograph by Robert Adams, a photographer whose work Lopez deeply respects. The picture takes the viewer's eye from the porch of an abandoned school house in Nebraska across Melvillean oceans of grass to a distant horizon of hills. The viewer is reminded of Lopez's abiding regard for uninterrupted open spaces on which the imagination can feast, take root and flourish.

As with the first two short story books, in the subtitle, *The Grace Note of the Canyon Wren,* is a bird which plays a totemic role. The wren in general is considered very clever. One myth explains how the wren surreptitiously obtained the title of King of Birds by secretly riding on the back of an eagle as it sought to fly the highest of all birds. When the eagle flew as high as it could, the wren hopped up and off its back, thereby securing the crown. Whether Lopez intended such a Trickster role is unlikely, given the subtitle's ethereal implications and the effervescence of the canyon wren's falling trill.

This book begins, like *Desert Notes* and *River Notes,* with a story called "Introduction" and is aptly subtitled "Within

Birds' Hearing." In this story, a nameless Desert Father on a pilgrimage to the ocean has traveled on foot for nearly two weeks in the eastern Mojave. He is expiring from a thirst that is twofold. There is the spiritual thirst for which only an unconditional surrender to the natural world can quench, hence the individual quest. Then there is the physical need. To that end the narrator depends on "the unceasing kindness of animals." With intimations from a Jesuit heritage, mourning doves drop water into the mouth of the nearly unconscious narrator and anoint his eyes.

Continuing in his journey, the narrator chances upon pictographs and respectfully comments on a vanished people in that "they loved, that they were afraid." Having opened his spiritual/physical self to what the landscape has to teach, the narrator hears the grace note of the canyon wren. Its falling trill leads him not during the day but more significantly at night—which might be considered the twilight region of the human psyche—to the "[h]eadwaters of the Oso," a station on his way, where he feels "the running tide of my own salted blood" in the water.

Lopez's genius at providing imaginative counterpoints to the archetypal terrors of the human psyche can be found in other stories in this book. An anchorite's mysterious but reverent lifestyle in "Teal Creek" ironically reaffirms the narrator's choice to actively participate in a peopled world. In his quest to determine what "kept the world from flying apart," he quietly acknowledges how a reading aloud of Native American stories comforts his daughter and him. Their "disarming morality" makes daughter and father "feel as if nothing would go wrong." In "Empira's Tapestry," the owner of a boarding house in a rural community has her complacency dispelled when a young female boarder doesn't let past disappointments nor life's unfairness keep her from savoring the beauty of the world. Their friendship becomes timeless when the narrator is invited by Empira to tell her "grandfather's stories of Ohio and the Great Plains" that she had "committed to memory." Once again, the reader is quietly reminded that we are custodians of stories. Their retellings can transform our worldview and help us transcend life's vagaries. The narrator in "The Entreaty of the Wiideema" intuits, by living with a formerly unknown aboriginal tribe in Australia, that stories shield us "in a different way from the fatal paradoxes of life."

Desert Fathers who take the long view in their relationships with others as well as with local landscapes and who serve as journey helpers wear many masks in Lopez's fiction. Their actions exhibit a moral intent even if their approach is humanly flawed such as the anchorite's penchant for monastic seclusion in "Teal Creek."

Selected for *Year's Best Fantasy and Horror 1995,* "The Entreaty of the Wiideema" returns to a favorite topic of Lopez's, namely, reminding the reader that the first step in taking the cultural pulse of indigenous peoples is to abandon stereotypes. In this story, the narrator is an anthropologist delivering a presentation about his two-and-a-half year sojourn with the Wiideema, a so-called primitive people in northern Australia. His stuttering demeanor, much like that of the anthropologist in "Winter Count 1973: Geese, They Flew Over in a Storm," effectively evokes a humility that evolved through his interactions with a non-Western culture.

He begins by acknowledging how he had to initially face the age-old ethical dilemma of deciding whether to "disturb these people if they are, indeed, there"—quietly existing in harmony with their surroundings in a remote region free of technological intrusion. To enter their culture, he has to put aside the Western, scientific method and forsake "menacing curiosity" for acute observation. His pompous feelings of techno-superiority are dwarfed by the Wiideema in a duel of cultures. When the narrator attempts to intimidate Karratumanta by starting a fire with a hand glass, Karratumanta one-ups him by stoning a songlark on the wing and eating "its two minute slabs of pectoral flesh." By succumbing to the Wiideema culture, the narrator begins to communicate with them in "the way a bird speaks or a creek, as a fish speaks or wind rushes in the grass." Eventually, the narrator comes to the non-Western conclusion that "companionship with the Wiideema, not reason, not explanation" is enough. In concluding his talk, the narrator expresses a desire "to understand now what it means to provide," another hallowed refrain of Lopez's.

Challenging cultural stereotypes and shattering complacencies are Lopezean specialties. "The Negro in the Kitchen" involves a black man, on an odyssey from Connecticut to the Pacific, who invites himself into the home of a health-obsessive white man. Any thoughts of a stereotypical confrontation between the haves and have-nots jackknifes in the reader's mind, as the sublime irony of the intruder's presence is revealed. Steal he does, but all he "robs" the white man of is a middle-class complacency. Both men are highly successful investment consultants, but whereas one is preoccupied with life-lists the other has a desire "to travel intimately across the country, to flow beautifully over the land, making very little disturbance." The black man leaves but not before he has sown seeds of discontent in the white man, who "put on another cup of coffee, which I never do after breakfast" and begins rereading a section on the Ruby-crowned kinglet.

"Homecoming" is a paradoxical title. Behind the story is an echoing theme that there is no "home" to come back to when intimacy with the land is lost. In this story, a botany graduate student, Wick Colter, has his career launched when he serendipitously joins a university field trip to Peru and subsequently publishes an article on "the evolutionary biology of Comistelliacae," a so-called elusive family among taxonomists. Colter's success is mercurial. He travels internationally, secures a coveted position at a local university and publishes widely.

Something happens to Colter, though. He loses his connection with the land and his family. He can't remember the names of plants in his own backyard, whereas previously he could identify them "by their shadows, how they dipped in the wind." He has no time for his family. His work becomes unsatisfying to him. In a sense, Colter has embarked on the three steps to Hell as identified by the father of the Jesuits, St. Ignatio of Loyola: money, power and pride. It takes a no-holds barred discussion with his wife for Colter to realize his folly. In contrition, Colter apologizes first to his wife and daughter. Then, taking Haskins' *Wild Flowers of the Pacific Coast,* he goes into the night and apologizes openly to the plants for having neglected them.

Taking animals for granted has even more haunting consequences. "Pearyland" evokes a dream kingdom where hunted animals' souls linger as they await rituals of gratefulness from the hunters who have killed them. "Only when that gift is completed" can the deceased animals re-inhabit the landscape and continue the cycle. "Lessons from the Wolverine" took twenty years to evolve. Its plot initially had wolverines speaking to Congress during the Vietnam War, "about human destructiveness and stupid behavior." Later, the plot developed into a dream landscape in which wolverines inform a hunter as to why they forbid hunting in the Ruby Mountains. The narrator dreams four times about wolverines in a desire "to be near animals until they showed you something that you didn't imagine" previously.

Narrators who do connect with their natural surroundings appear more vibrant, possess bountiful insights and are privileged to experience what Lopez refers to as *agape,* "a kind of love... between [you] and the place." In "The Open Lot," Jane Weddell "saw no greater purpose in life than to reveal and behold," as she prepared fossils in the Museum of Natural History. Glenn Wycliff is an esthete, not unlike Henry David Thoreau or Sierra Club founder, John Muir, who hears the boom of "church bells buried beneath" windblown sand in "Sonora." Mirara has "given herself away to the place, and it's how it responds to her" as ancient trails reveal themselves to her as she runs effortlessly throughout the Grand Canyon in "The Runner."

Field Notes: The Grace Note of the Canyon Wren marks a significant achievement in Lopez's development as a writer. His stories thrive on many levels. Foremost, they entertain without exploiting violence or sexuality. Violence occurs rarely and is incidental to the storyline. The take-home messages in these short stories remain constant but are more subliminal than those in *Desert Notes* or *River Notes*.

Discussion of a Lopezean story is better suited to an inquiry rather than to any conclusion. His short stories defy definition and have no literary bottom. The stories are open-ended, flush with understatement and weave through multiple dimensions simultaneously. To this end, one story's title, "Conversation," was first seen in *Desert Notes*. Lopez trusts his readers, invites their imaginations to partake of the stories' synergistic possibilities and acknowledges that even he cannot fathom all that is coursing through the veins of imagery and circumstances that have been rendered. Complexity and refinement dominate this book. One critic wrote that Lopez "leaves all the right things unsaid, and the silence resonates." Another described these stories as tales "of solitude, contemplation, and grace."

Light Action in the Caribbean (2000) is a book of thirteen short stories that should have received one of literature's most coveted awards. Its stylistic fluency belies the underpinnings of an imaginative complexity that only a master craftsman could realize.

Within these pages, Lopez causes time to loop, cultural boundaries to disintegrate and collective memory to foster guardianships. Newcomers to Lopez's short stories will welcome the exotic, intricately woven plot lines and character developments that occur in relatively few pages and limited time frames. As enthusiastic as readers might be to consume several short stories at one sitting, they might feel preoccupied as they unconsciously process and synthesize the particulars of a previously read story. Aficionados will be incited by the creative manifestations of Lopez's life-long quests and ought to recognize semblances of favorite characters from earlier works. Scholars will be reminded of Joseph Campbell's *The Hero with a Thousand Faces*.

Lopez continues to simultaneously publish award-winning, anthology-destined works of both fiction and nonfiction. In 1995, he received an award in fiction from the Pacific Northwest Booksellers. *About This Life* (1998) nimbly engages the intimacy of the memoir form to examine issues facing mankind in the 21st century. Magazine-published articles and essays are regularly featured in specialty book publications: *Best American Essays; Best Spiritual Writing; American Nature Writing; Best of Outside, The First Twenty Years; From the Field: A Book of Writings from National Geographic* and *Writers' Harvest*. His fiction appears continuously on short lists for a variety of awards: "Thomas Lowdermilk's Generosity" for Distinguished Stories of 1993, "Remembering Orchards" for a PEN Syndicated Fiction Award and "The Letters of Heaven" as finalist for the National Magazine Award in Fiction. A third honorary L.H.D. was presented to Lopez in 2000 by Texas Tech University.

Light Action in the Caribbean was initially entitled *The Letters of Heaven*, but changed upon Lopez realizing how "new work helped [him] understand much more about the organization of the book." A Lannan Residency Fellowship in 1999 assisted in its completion. No photographs or drawings accompany these short stories. Reference to a bird in the subtitle is also absent, but part of one does appear on the dust jacket. Intriguingly, the bird appears to be an artist's rendition depicting the bottom half of a perching, parrot-like bird from the macaw family. The coloration suggests it is a scarlet macaw, "perhaps from Venezuela," that the narrator describes in "Mornings in Quarain." Generally, the macaw is large, vibrantly colorful in numerous hues and an endangered species due to loss of habitat and poaching. Whether Lopez intended the "disappearing" macaw on the dust jacket to be allegorical is speculative yet plausible considering how intricately interactive each short story book is.

The detail and care with which this book unfolded is a story in itself. At one point, two stories were pulled and the sequence revisited by Lopez from "the sense that those two stories didn't quite fit and the others interfered with each other's effect in the earlier order." A Pushcart Prize recipient, "Benjamin Claire, North Dakota Tradesman, Writes to the President of the United States," was omitted. "Emory Bear Hands' Birds" had already been published in *Island,* an Australian magazine, when Lopez determined the story "had gotten away from me." The version in this book is the revised one, later published in *San Francisco* magazine. The changes are minor but significant in how they affect the flow of the story. For Lopez, every word, every sound matters to the ecology of the piece. He appreciates how even an adjective can trickle through a paragraph to shrewdly influence tone and impact. The changes in "Emory Bear Hands' Birds" might be considered incidental but to a master wordsmith like Lopez they are quintessential.

Lopez's "telling of beautiful untrue things" routinely exhausts the parameters of reality. Within the quotidian of these short stories breathes a tone of real-life innuendo that caused one serious reader to declare that "Remembering

Orchards" had to be a memoir. The plots for "Stolen Horses" and "The Deaf Girl" have the earmarks of news articles but are not. "Ruben Mendoza Vega," with its extensive footnotes and bibliography, defies categorization. "In the Garden of the Lords of War" yokes language suggestive of mythology. Narrators in "Emory Bear Hands' Birds," "The Letters of Heaven" and "The Construction of the Rachel" matter-of-factly relate improbable events that are all the more convincing due to their nonfictive cast. In all these short stories, details are realistically informative yet unadorned.

Light Action is vintage Lopez in the usual life-affirming ways, but it also unleashes a series of baneful events that are not softened by metaphor, will likely haunt rather than reassure the reader and may herald yet another literary landscape for an author who is undaunted by complex issues. A theme of old-fashioned reckoning permeates three stories which disclose disheartening aspects of humankind. "The Deaf Girl," "Stolen Horses" and "Light Action in the Caribbean" appear post-apocalyptic in their savagery and portray a series of plots which, on the surface, seem inimical to Lopez's usual venues. Prior to these three stories, violence has been incidental, non-graphic and allegorical. In earlier books, unspeakable wrongdoing was held to metaphor in such stories as "Lessons from the Wolverine," whereby both wolverine and wolf suffer hideous deaths due to a depraved indifference by a trapper who, in turn, could represent mindless human mischief. These three *Light Action* stories speak of displaced people with displaced souls, reminding readers of what might be inevitable when cultures fragment and their inhabitants wander in a moral wasteland.

In "The Deaf Girl," Dalamina is a twelve-year-old whose family forsakes California for the elusive sanctuary of Montana, after a "stray bullet one night in Long Beach" leaves her deaf. In what might be regarded as a sign of the times, she is brutally violated by a local teenager who has been corrupted by television and who is mesmerized by the random violence that had caused Dalamina's deafness. After the assault, the story takes a Lopezean twist. Dalamina intends to confront her tormentor like Lopez's animistic avatars have always done. In the process, she subsequently challenges human complacency by blazing a trail of righteous indignation that pulls the smug narrator in its wake. Although much younger and less worldly than the narrator, she possesses a wisdom beyond her years and limited experience. Raped and left for dead, Dalamina raises her bloody, abused body to stalk her attacker and force him to acknowledge his harm upon her "until he makes a mess in his pants. For him, that's going to be the beginning." Hers is a virtuous wrath of the living dead. She is a voice from the grave come back to plague the tormentor. In cryptic understatement, the reader is left to imagine what earthly purgatory awaits her assailant.

The narrator's point of view in "Stolen Horses" arises from an act of indiscretion. There is an undercurrent that the horses in this story, like many natural resources Lopez writes of, are refugees caught in mankind's never-ending cultural crossfires. On the story's surface, several local bad boys exhibit an irrational, callused anger when their inheritance is seemingly squandered. Their parents' ranches have been sold to investors "waving big money around." The disenfranchised youths rustle horses "on these three-hundred-acre, new-money show places" for eventual sale to investors back East who think their newly acquired wealth entitles them to a piece of the Old West.

On another plain, vexation spawns from the narrator's outrage that land his family had known intimately, having "ranched that central Oregon country for four generations," will be in the hands of people who did not know "even literally which way the wind blew." In yet another sphere, the narrator acknowledges the theft of land by his forefathers from the Molala, whose anguish must have matched his own. The horse rustling venture is lucrative and appears risk free. The gang of four's spin of the wheel of poetic justice quickly becomes farcical. An attempt to rustle horses in the starlight goes awry and murder occurs. The narrator escapes the fate of his accomplices. His cohorts don't rat him out. Unwittingly, he had released the stolen horses before slinking away. His mindless act mitigates the robbery charges and lessens jail bids for two of the young outlaws. Twelve years later, the narrator leads a respectable life in Florida with his wife and children who do not suspect his criminal past. Inwardly, he knows there is a reckoning that almost seems to beckon. He inhabits a spiritual hell while waiting for that dreadful knock on the door that would be his undoing.

The title story, "Light Action in the Caribbean," ripples with surface tension. Its savage ending may catch the reader off-guard by a stylistic omission that lacks the usual connective tissue for reconciliation and/or redemption. The plot's internal struggle is unusual for Lopez. In no other short story book of his is the conflict of man versus man so overt or unsettling.

Two scuba diving vacationers from Colorado fly to the island resort of San Carlos where they pay for the trip of their lives with their lives. Libby Dalaria is a vacuous young lady who is misguided about matters of the heart. Her boyfriend, David, is a very ugly American with a high-tech job whose need to manipulate ultimately sets the stage for tragedy. Both have been seduced into believing that nothing can go wrong with their vacation plans, given David's penchant for being "in *command* of [his] universe" and everyone else's. Contrasted to David's crassness is Esteban, a local who owns a Boston Whaler that once served his father for subsistence fishing and now serves him in the tourist trade. Part of the package deal David has prearranged is for five days of exclusive use of Esteban and his boat. Esteban shows his mettle in several ways. Throughout the day, he manages to sidestep David's bantering and badgering. He is satisfied to make a living rather than the fortune David predicts would be his upon evolving into the electronic business world. While Libby and David are diving, he avoids dropping the anchor, which would damage the fragile coral. And he stands his ground upon insisting that David toss endangered conchs back into the water: "Put dem over, mon. Drop dem in."

The reader is lulled into believing he will be left with characteristic nuances lapping gently against his skull, when a pirate vessel runs down the fleeing whaler. What happens next is a gruesome description of the murders of Esteban, Libby and David. The depravity in which the latter two are brutally raped and the practiced manner in which all three are strapped to concrete footings to be dumped ignominiously into the ocean is so realistic it is nauseating. The reader catches a glimpse of what might loom ahead when a global economy fueled by so-called technological advances unwittingly breeds sociopathic tendencies.

Other stories in this book remind the reader of the power of love, forgiveness and reconciliation. Devoted readers will recognize more intricate versions of earlier narrators, such as the uncommon gardener in "The Lover of Words" who is not unlike Thomas Lowdermilk. In "Thomas Lowdermilk's Generosity," which *Best American Short Stories* included on its Distinguished Stories list in 1994, a landscape artist rises above malicious gossip that initially cripples his ability to love and to be curious. Only when he learns to tap into the rejuvenating strength that radiates from his wife's devotion to him and from the goodness in people does his wholeness return. In "Emory Bear Hands' Birds," inmates who sought "the counsel of [their] totem animals" were prayed into birds that flew to northern

Montana where they would live out their lives in freedom "along the Marias River." "Remembering Orchards" echoes a recurring theme when the death of a parent prompts self-examination and, ultimately, life-affirmation. A stepson's grief is dissipated when he acknowledges how the orchard tending hands of his stepfather "sleep in my hands," whenever he engages in his craft of setting type.

"Mornings in Quarain" also involves the death of a parent but addresses complex social and cultural issues. Frances Amelia Desuedeson is an articulate, free-spirited Western woman who has made her home in the Middle East and is viewed as a dangerous interloper. She wears "long pants and travel[s] as a Christian." Her appearance of effrontery and her published articles about "birds and sand dunes" galvanize the ire of zealots. The narrator arrives in Riyadh, Saudi Arabia to collect the manuscripts and diaries of his mother who was murdered over seven years earlier by "reactionary fanatics who rigged the gas explosion in her kitchenette." The mother's crime, it seems, was her pluck to write intimately and with passion about a culture she was not born into. The corollary between her dilemma and that of Lopez's is transparent, although it is unlikely the author intended that message. Lopez has been unduly criticized for blending elements of Native American cultures in his writings. Not unlike the heroine in this story, Lopez writes with humility, enthusiasm and respect for cultures other than his own.

"The Letters of Heaven" is a riveting story that was on *The Best American Short Stories* list for Distinguished Stories in 1998. Irrespective of the story's religious overtones, its marrow contains one of Lopez's most hallowed refrains, i.e., to preserve the stories that protect us from life's terrors and which remind us of our own possibilities. Similar to Abu-Said in "Quarain," who acted as an intermediary for the preservation of exquisite but inflammatory papers, the narrator in "Letters" is tormented by blasphemy. For Ramón they involve illicit letters between two unlikely instruments of grace who were canonized. As a teenager he surreptitiously discovers what he considers to be sordid correspondence between Martin de Porres and Rosa de Flores, written nearly four hundred years earlier in Lima, Peru. His guilt is exacerbated by his own emerging sexuality and the knowledge that he is a descendant of Rosa's brother.

In mid-life, Ramón chances across another set of their letters and undergoes "a spiritual revolution" upon acknowledging "their humanity, the fearless, complete acceptance of passion." Reminiscent of ancient, hierophanous events that transcend earthly experience, Martin and Rosa's sexual rapture "intensified rather than quenched the light of God." Through their spiritual revelations, they became imbued with an immeasurable charity toward the most abject and brutalized victims of "the Spanish viceroyalty" during "a period of human derangement." A cosmic rapport emanated from Martin and Rosa and manifested in miraculous ways. He learned to speak with animals. They were often seen elevated "off the ground before the Crucifix in a state of spiritual ecstasy." Ramón's spiritual ecdysis yields a world-view and awakens him to the ubiquity of the divine in all gestures. In supplication and to preserve whatever sublime possibilities the letters suggest, he plots their publication.

Loss and reconciliation are motifs that occur in "The Construction of the Rachel." The narrator takes refuge in a monastery upon being informed by his wife that she has met someone else. Unlike the narrator in "Homecoming," the estrangement is complete. He builds a miniature "square-rigged, three-masted ship" from flotsam that washes up on the beach in a manner remindful of Lopez's impulse to take life's debris and ingeniously craft it into kaleidoscopic life-maps. When the miniature ship is launched in the ocean, the reader will not be shocked to realize it becomes life-sized and is boarded by the narrator and the monastic anchorites, who "were adaptable and willing, and lived lives of belief."

Two stories in particular provide templates for living a life with moral intent. They also encapsulate many Lopezean tenets. "In the Garden of the Lords of War," which was selected for *Best American Nature Writing 1997*, is ironically about peace. Its setting occupies a futuristic landscape that explains how virtuous men and women have avoided other wars after the Universal Holocaust. Technology is non-existent nor is there any sense of materialistic desire. All forms of fanaticism are discouraged. Living in harmony with the land; moving with the seasons; learning and appreciating other cultures; loving and being loved, as well as avoiding that which is unnecessary, are crucial elements in maintaining a cross-cultural chemistry that "starved, angered, and humiliated the dogs of war." In "The Mappist," apprentice and journeyman meet when a restoration geographer becomes obsessed with the implications of what an eighty-eight year old cartographer is attempting to do. In an effort to preserve each state's natural history and human involvement "of the place from Native American times," Corlis Benefideo is systematically identifying information that "shows history and how people fit the places they occupy." Predictably, Benefideo is opposed to "the venality of material wealth" and, therefore, excludes man-made excesses such as shopping malls. His intention is to inventory the priceless landscape and to create a system for doing the same worldwide. How Benefideo and Lopez "understand the world is through natural history, geography, and anthropology." In a handing down of values, the narrator explains that his daughter desires to be an environmental historian so as "to discover the kind of information you need to have to build a stable society." The story ends the book, like other books have, with a quiet bid to the reader to now take what he has learned and to accept the satisfying burden of protecting the irreplaceable in his own backyard.

The stories in *Light Action in the Caribbean* profile many

Lopezean axioms while embarking on the classic tradition of questing in previously uncharted terrain where the outcomes are uncertain. Russell Banks hailed these stories as "tough-minded, emotionally turbulent, and always intelligent." E. Annie Proulx called them "subtle and mysterious" and predicted that no reader could leave them unchanged. Robert Draper wrote that the book "is full of delicate pleasures."

Resistance (2004) earned the H.L. Davis Award for Short Fiction, which has been given annually since 1987 to an Oregon writer. No other short story book is more fully integrated or compelling in physical layout, style or refrain. The dust jacket depicts a replication of the hard cover constrained by a taut wrapping of rubber bands. Whether their restriction is symbolic invites consideration. Lopez dedicated the book to his wife's four daughters in "admiration for their politics and determination." An Alan Magee monotype precedes each of nine short stories. Magee's provocative titles can be located on the copyright page. Like the sublime in Lopez's fiction, they prickle the archetypal.

Lopez's seamless deliveries now approach the invisible and continue to involve an imperceptible blend of techniques that invigorate the reader's imagination. Many have become signatures within a style that is presented with the fluency of a master storyteller. Prose still pulsates with rhythm and meter. Characters continue to engage in internal dialogues through the first person singular pronoun, as they wrangle with man versus self conflicts that suggest quest motifs. Most convincingly, Lopez humanizes them by showing the reader their clay feet. Despite aspirations for social change, they must navigate through the usual conceits and calamities that harry everyone. The conversational tone remains diffident and of a confidential nature. Suspense is aroused through discrete asides. Nothing is embellished. The reader is trusted like a lifelong friend who can find his way through nuance. Understatement stirs unconscious impulses. Haiku-like images approach the status of koans as they express the paradoxical, the inexpressible and the incomprehensible.

Resistance embodies many of Lopez's tenets, eloquently expressed in his earlier works of fiction and nonfiction. What is striking about this volume is the articulation of an apocalyptic crisis in our country that is not unlike those that have plagued other cultures since antiquity. Humankind's inability to reap wisdom from erstwhile events foreshadows cycles of needless misery for future generations. In no earlier short story book has Lopez engaged in such a sustained creative effort with a social theme so starkly exposed. A reader might point to fiction like "Conversation" from *Field Notes,* "Benjamin Claire," "Lessons from the Wolverine" or "The Mappist" and to nonfiction like *The Rediscovery of North America* as being likely progenitors. Reference could be made to a time in the 1970s when Lopez's sense of "civil disobedience" caused him to harbor a draft resister who opposed the Viet Nam war, which urged "A Quiet Voice in the Wilderness." Not without some measure of influence might be Lopez's immersion in current social issues "since the Florida [presidential] election debacle" of 2000. What is extraordinary about this short story book is the artfulness in which Lopez is able to remind a reader "that community, not the individual, is the basic building block for a healthy society."

"Apocalypse" raises the bar in its time-honored condemnation of any institution that would squander the imaginative juices of its citizens under the pretext of protecting them. It sets the mood for a series of short stories that chronicle a new generation of expatriates. According to Lopez, the reader must begin with this story so as "to get the setup first in order to understand completely the stories that follow." Through the story's protagonist, Owen, we learn that former college classmates refuse to become victims of either personal trauma or of their country's adolescent self-absorption, choosing instead to channel their gifts as "writers, artists and scholars" into social activism. They pursue lives with moral intent in far-flung reaches of the globe. Until they are targeted by an "Investigator of Moral Climates" of "a repressive United States government," none of them realize that their search for "proportion in life, a pattern of grace" is heresy to a culture that demands its masses indulge in "an appetite for distraction."

The story opens with reference to a letter that is unsettling but whose prophetic contents are not disclosed until Owen explains the disillusionment that caused many of his former classmates to disown a country supersaturated with compulsive spin doctors and with "people who celebrate the insults of advertising." Having come to the realization that "what endures is simple devotion to the question of having been alive," they seek "the histories of other, older cultures." Stalwart as Owen is to ideals that may suggest a warrior's demeanor, his character is made accessible to the reader through emotional vulnerability. When Owen confides in the reader about an intangible fear that he and Mary might accidentally succumb to estrangement "by tides we don't recognize," the reader can readily recognize and perhaps identify with Owen.

From this background emerge transparent parallels that involve America's current totalitarian excesses and which echo classical works that encourage a grass roots response to totalitarianism. A few include "On Civil Disobedience" by Henry David Thoreau, *The Iron Heel* by Jack London, *WE* by Yevgeny Zamyatin, *1984* by George Orwell, and *Fahrenheit 451* by Ray Bradbury. Regrettably, a reader who is polarized by "Apocalypse" might become overly distracted from the poetic implications of the following eight stories which, strategically, focus on emotional survival and, ultimately, reconciliation with personal demons.

Interestingly, the Magee image that prefaces "Apocalypse" is entitled "Writer's Mask." It would be whimsical to suggest that Owen is Lopez in creative disguise. The story's tone may be vestigial to *The Rediscovery of North America* and to similar indictments against our consumer-obsessive society. Lopez might even "love what Owen Daniels says at the end of his story." And the peripheral intimations of a primeval, menacing presence do resurrect from his earliest fiction. What might be more intriguing is whether this story is a vessel for an embodiment of unequivocal truths that Lopez humbly acknowledges are accesible to all artists, not just writers, and which cause their works to be timeless and to have universal appeal. If, through Owen, Lopez has tapped into a "quiet elucidation of those civic priniciples, which are so easy to subscribe to," perhaps all of humankind has an Owen in their genetic code.

What Owen expresses so passionately and convincingly is only alluded to in the following eight stories. This is a skillful maneuver by Lopez. It gives the reader respite from what could otherwise devolve into rhetoric. It invites the reader to vicariously join a protagonist like Jefferson deShay from "Laguna de Bay in A-Sharp" in wincing at youthful self-righteousness. It also provides the reader with a sampler of global venues in which Western-trained minds do yield to "the histories of other, older cultures."

Two stories in particular pull on remnants of the durability of Native American cultures, while laying open the forlornity of those who "lead lives of quiet desperation." Not unlike the unnamed protagonist in "The Bend" from *River Notes,* who "dismantled [his] loneliness" upon acknowledging the spiritual ecology of his own beingness in an integrated world, their main characters squabble with a fundamental disconnect.

In "The Bear in the Road," Edward Larmirande is bewildered by an inability to access what is decidedly his totem animal, the grizzly bear. Since childhood his perceptions of the world have been informed by Virgil Night Crow, an Assiniboine, who initially assumes a grandfatherly role in conveying "practical things—finding water, tracking animals, which cactus fruits were okay to eat." Inexplicably, at age fifteen, when Edward is left "alone for four days to fast and dream" at the confluence of two wilderness creeks in Montana, his vision quest is rebuffed. Not until his second attempt, over twelve years and several bear encounters later, does he begin to exhibit the ironic subtlety in which he inherited his "father's scorn for ideas." Despite Virgil's guiding hand, Edward "would not give in to" what Lopez describes as the numinous or divine presence of a place. His unwillingness to hear "the rustling and voices of animals that had lived in this place long ago" kept them at arm's length. It takes six more years before Edward is able to return to the "same camp above the dry creek bed." Thankfully, he is able to silence the contentious noises inside himself and, in doing so, defer to the oldest culture of all.

As with many other stories by Lopez, this one's potency lies in techniques that are meek in their delivery. Virgil's role as indigenous journey helper/mentor allows him to advance staples earmarked in much earlier stories: "how one small thing signaled another," how you must "pay attention," how through memory "everything, even the buffalo, is still around" and how "you have to keep telling the stories." The character of Edward is enjoined to remark "how [the land] had emptied out" of wildlife, with speculation about human gluttony that circles back to "Pearyland" and "Lessons from the Wolverine" in *Field Notes*. Mention of his "seeing some young woman pull over to drag a dead animal off the road" hearkens Lopez's own gentle reverence for our "animal" brethren as expressed in *Apologia*. Regardless of the protagonist's appearance of a privileged socio-economic status he is kept on a level playing field with any reader who must endure the tragic death, the infidelity or the estrangement of a beloved parent. Authenticity is incrementally established through the casual familiarity in which place names like "Porcupine Creek" or "Hi-line" and landscape terms like "escarpment," "borrow ditch," "doab," "buttes" or "coulee" are referred to. Almost a footnote mention is made about a volatile topic that may have roots in Lopez's nonfiction book about wolves. The Montana ranchers' "God-given right to go after a stock-killing bear" echoes an unenlightened sentiment expressed in *Of Wolves and Men* and mimics our founding fathers' Christian abhorrence of Nature, as expressed in Roderick Nash's *Wilderness and the American Mind*. Not without intrigue is the stone-skipping mini-lesson on modern instances of global genocide, which is offset by mention of a bibliotherapeutic reading list that provides role-models for resisting oppression.

"Nílch´i," which is Navajo for Holy Wind, reminds the reader how "all one's efforts are bent toward enhancing and balancing the experience of feeling included in life." Marion's search for meaning causes the usual familial anguish, beginning in adolescence and extending to his own wife and children. Years earlier, graduate studies in anthropology had allowed him to tap into the rich diversity of "human social arrangements" that are widespead and enduring. To this he returns after a failed marriage. Marion then recounts the "Navajo belief [that] winds exist all around and also within a person," treating the reader to another culture's way of staying in harmony with one's self and society. Unlike Edward, whose vision quest was accessible in his cultural backyard, Marion embarks on a worldwide journey so as to experience "the longest-known and most dependable of the earth's winds." Maybe, then, he will be able to fulfill an earlier ambition to "leave no trace of [his] passing" on terrains he floats across.

Intimacy with a particular landscape might be stereotyped as a birthright only bestowed after a few generations of its denizens have roamed a locale. Not so with Lopez's characters. From his earliest short story books, the numina of unfamiliar places have been actively sought by characters whose humble desire is reverential participation that suggests spiritual cleansing and renewal. Marion is not unlike the cross-country traveler from "The Negro in the Kitchen" in *Field Notes,* who would "flow beautifully over the land, making very little disturbance." Nor is he far removed from the sojourner, in "The Hot Spring" of *Desert Notes,* who "looked across the desert and imagined that he had come to life again."

The book's most fully actualized persona might be "Caucasian, and a woman from the West" in "The Walls at Yogpar," who immerses herself in China's myriad languages, cultures and geographies. Elizabeth's enthusiasm propels her into mainstream Chinese life. Her "desire for unbounded physical space, an open geography" pulls her into its most remote and human-free regions. Not surprisingly, a disdain for emerging corporate greed causes her to forgo lucrative translation assignments in favor of recording the stories of interesting, older women and of preserving "Urumchi street slang." Lopez quietly brings home the intrinsic richness of local language/knowledge, when Elizabeth acquires "a book of landscape terms in Uygur" and then ruminates over provocative geographic subtleties. Through her the reader encounters staggering facts about the country's vastness and fascinating historical asides about the disappearance of "original evidence for Peking man," of the ritual burial of a child sixty-five thousand years earlier and—in a sobering parallel to America—of nuclear weapons test sites in so-called wastelands. Elizabeth's inner serenity seems to well from the land's own sense of equanimity, especially from its ancestral spirits that still dwell there. Not without intrigue is the Magee monotype that precedes this story, which is entitled "Spirit" and which graces the cover of *Resistance*'s French edition.

Not to be overlooked is how these holdovers from the value-clarifying '60s share similar ethics, not just with one another but with all others on the planet who cherish community over material acquisition. Likewise, they undergo similar epiphanies, independently of one another, "to be vigilant and to seek loving relationships." Common needs universally expressed—to feel useful, to cause as little harm as possible, to celebrate/participate fully in the "theologies of creation"— inform their actions. Of no small consequence is the spiritual centering that radiates from their connecting/reconnecting with the numinous in landscapes. Not lost on the reader is exposure to the complex simplicities of "other, older cultures" that offer beneficent alternatives to hubris and venality.

What distinguishes the following main characters is their resolve to fully re-engage in life-affirming activities, upon weathering soul-shattering nightmares that have released toxins into the fabric of their beings. In "Rio de la Plata," Lisa's professional success as a highly sought-after architect is, ultimately, unfulfilling. She cultivates a social aloofness that alienates potential suitors and reduces friendships to acquaintances. Even with pro bono work, "something crucial in [her] would not engage." Worse still, Lisa feels she has betrayed the ideals of her youth. She never really became a bulwark against social injustice. Her spiritual disintegration finally halts when she devours premises expressed in a book her dying mother hands her, amid the revelation that her parents met "in Bergen-Belsen, fourteenth of July, 1943."

Gary's own "triumph over despair" occurs in a more visceral way. Vivid memories of childhood sexual abuse have built walls around his heart. His inability to receive unconditional love does not keep him from leading a satisfactory life as a cabinetmaker. Like the persona in Emerson's poem *Forbearance*, who has "at rich men's tables eaten bread and pulse," so is Gary welcomed into homes on four continents. Any sensations of self-pity are allayed by the street misery he encounters. The violence inflicted on him was "a kind of instruction" that now instills empathy toward anyone "for whom harm never slept." Unexplainably, Gary's emotional walls begin to crumble while he is staying with a family in Bangalore. His host's young daughter spontaneously kisses his forehead in a gesture of bidding good night. Further crumbling follows his cathartic lashing out at a street waif who attacks him with a knife. Through his host's tacit comments and expressions of genuine concern, Gary chooses not to respond as a victim might to injustice. The assailant sees a healer after his prison bid and, early one day, unceremoniously drops off "salvaged teak wood." Months later Gary marvels at how his inner rage has withered. He contemplates the Japanese folktale about a brown bear that knows which roots to select so as to heal a wound. Recalling the story awakens Gary's longing to reunite with the female acquaintance who "lived near Abashiri in northern Hokkaido."

In "Traveling with Bo Ling," Harvey is another character who learns "to wash out the anger" by succumbing to love. That includes being intoxicated by a peach's "summer juice running down [his] bare chest," if he would "not be [among] the martyred slaves of Time." Harvey and Bo Ling were married more than two decades after he came home from the Viet Nam war. Both have been brutalized unmercifully. Harvey was blinded during a firefight that also turned his face waxen and burned away his penis/scrotum. Bo Ling had lye poured into her face by a jealous husband who had brought her to California. For the first two years of their marriage, Harvey and Bo Ling inhabit a no man's land of bitterness and rage. A theme central to the book emerges when Harvey is told by his father, a WWII veteran, that war's lesson is to teach us "to be vigilant." Through Harvey's monologues, the reader is solicited to consider whether we as a species are addicted to "the forbidden pleasure of violence." In counterpoint, by way of Bo Ling's coaxings, the reader is reminded of the surest way to access life's joys. It begins by not allowing emotional and/or physical handicaps to be self-defining/limiting. Harvey and Bo Ling take "the geographic cure." They begin with a trip to Bo Ling's North Vietnamese village, where the ex-GI is received without rancor. Other travels in the next several years unveil innocent pleasures so liberating that these most unlikely "honeymooners" embrace what might become their ultimate expression of life-affirmation—adopting a child.

"Flight from Berlin" artfully coalesces many ideas pioneered in Lopez's earliest writings. A pivotal refrain is that "other, older cultures" hold remedies to intractable social ills specific to modern societies. "Flight" begins with a descriptive paragraph about the spring equinox along the Utala River in Brazil, where the American expat, Eric, lives among the Tukano people. Years earlier, he and his family fled an America that had broken faith with its most basic of premises—individual freedom. His wife dead "of dengue hemorrhagic fever eight years into it" and their children now grown and scattered, Eric has become a self-styled naturalist who learns "how to live 'quietly' in their part of the Curiouriari River country." True to character, Eric presents to the reader a convincing rendition of indigenous animals and plants that includes winsome asides about our palliative need for "putting the face to a flower" and "drawing by dialogue." From this equatorial Innisfree where Eric has "been restored," the reader is given pause when Eric recounts a story once told to him by a woman attending a conference in Beirut. Long after her grandfather had survived Treblinka, he "became a docent in a museum there." Without explaining his past connection to the death camp, he would ask visitors "to be vigilant, or it would come again." When a female from Buenos Aires yells "¡Nunca mas!" ("Never Again!"), in reference to the "30,000 killed during military rule [in Argentina] between 1976 and 1983," the reader has to wince over government-sponsored slaughter among our global neighbors in Darfur, Iraq and Afghanistan. In an act of vigilance, Red Dragonfly Press recently published Lopez's ¡NUNCA MÁS! (2007), a fine press chapbook. His reflections upon the genocidal impulses in humankind propose a citizen-based inquiry into "the question of genocide and slavery, upon which the Republic has been built."

Resistance is an artist's response to amoral conduct by the most powerful country in the history of humankind. Although this short story book was worthy of the Bellwether Prize in 2004, given annually for "socially responsible literature," Lopez was one of that year's judges. He is widely recognized as having advocated resistance to personal despair and to social injustice for decades. For him, the act of writing has always been "a social impulse." Given our govenment's sustained attack on the Bill of Rights and worldwide degradation of the planet's life-support systems, he believes "now, an artistic vision that doesn't reflect on human fate is self-indulgent." It would be gauche to describe Lopez as a luddite or to portray his protagonists as "true believers." Through Eric, the reader is cautioned against replacing one brand of fundamentalism for another, that the art of vigilance also involves being "careful not to declare any particular person or thing the enemy." Not lost on the reader are the sophisticated and complex artistic impulses that lubricate the ideas/ideals in these short stories. Simply put, they are delightful fables that celebrate the noblest of human desires. Jim Crace called Resistance "a work of luminous gravity" whose narratives "are daring, sensuous, beautiful, and important."

Home Ground:
Language for an American Landscape
Book Review

Home Ground: Language for an American Landscape. Edited by
Barry Lopez and Debra Gwartney. Trinity University Press.
October 2006. 449 pages with illustrations (oversized). $29.95.
ISBN-13: 978-1595-34024-5.

Unsure whether you are hiking in a *goat prairie* or up a *cowfaced
slope?* Can't find the right word to describe a water hole (try
kiss tank or *tinaja*). Unable to decide whether you are camping
on a *catstep*, a *bench* or a *terrace?* Vaguely recall "silt soft as a
Holstein's belly" *(cowbelly)* as you were learning to swim in the
cricks/kills/runs of rural America? Think that since your home
ground is a city then landscape terms are irrelevant... consider
Manhattan's Murray *Hill* or Central Park's *desire paths* and even
Hell's Kitchen. Would like a reference book whose physical layout heightens readability, whose language is plain-speaking with
a delectable blend of folklore, etymology, literary overtones and
illustrations, yet is scientifically accurate? Well, try *Home Ground,*
a catalogue of landscape terms and phrases that spawned when
its senior editor, Barry Lopez, winner of the National Book
Award in 1986 for *Arctic Dreams,* could not locate the origin or
meaning of *blind river.*

Readers will be pleasantly surprised to discover a few of
their favorite authors either listed among *Home Ground's* forty-
five contributors or whose work is alluded to so as to highlight
how a landscape term might aptly describe a particular place.
Within these pages are entries by Charles Frazier, Barbara
Kingsolver, Jon Krakauer and Terry Tempest Williams. Theirs'
and other writers' home grounds span the landscapes of

America and discuss terms as provocative as *buffalo jump* or *ice volcano* and as mellifluous as *kudzu* or *looking-glass prairie*. Each writer was awarded a group of twenty words, hand-picked for that particular writer and based in part on a word's relevance to that writer's home region. The writers were then tasked with a herculean amount of suggested background readings and encouraged to bring their unique imaginations to bear in the process of providing "what a reader needs to know," according to BL. This artistic freedom guaranteed a diversity and a richness that is unprecedented for what is ultimately a reference book. No entry is alike in tone or presentation, with lengths ranging from twenty-four words for Bill Kittredge's *finger drift* to 366 words for Trish Hampl's *lake*. A tireless team of researchers scoured a myriad of literary genres in their quest to find quintessential entry examples, while an advisory board of scientists waited in the wings to peruse each definition so as to preserve scientific integrity. BL may have been the senior editor, but "the work of producing the first clean, solid draft was Debra's alone." Thanks to her "three years of tactful negotiation between the writers and the board of advisors" these kindred spirits found common ground for an uncommon dictionary.

Home Ground is more than a dictionary of place. It offers a respite from a society where cell phones, iPods, Blackberries and GPS Navigators mischievously disconnect us from where we actually are. *Home Ground* revitalizes our sense of place and community. Much like the *Foxfire* series of the 1970s and, more recently, "the greatest generation" surge of stories surrounding WWII veterans, *Home Ground* reminds us of the cultural urgency of recording who we are. Acknowledging the specific names of locations where we live, where we love and where we raise our families reaffirms "a sense of allegiance with our chosen places." As BL humbly recalled, while speaking at the Northshire Bookstore in Manchester, VT during a twenty-city, whirlwind book tour for *Home Ground,* there is reciprocity in the landscapes we inhabit. Years ago, while he was traveling in a remote area, an indigenous elder noticed him appearing to be melancholy. Upon inquiry, he answered that he was homesick, to which she replied, "Your place is also missing you."

Readers who are familiar with BL's work will recognize one of his signature styles in how he views the writer's responsibility as being a companion to the reader, not an authority. *Home Ground* does not pretend to be definitive.

Of the original list of 1,500 terms a mere 848 became entries. There is both an inferred and an explicit invitation within these pages for the reader to actively participate. An expansive bibliography awaits all aficionados who wish either to retrace a contributor's journey or to track their own local terms. A contributors' section identifies published works for readers to delve into. For those curious about BL, his home page is **www.barrylopez.com**. Those who want to comment on an entry or who would like to contribute to future versions of *Home Ground* can reach editors at **www.homegroundproject.com**.

MN
Hartwick, NY
November 2006–February 2008

Epilogue

No Bottom focuses on Barry Lopez's short story books, while pulling on parallel concepts evident throughout his nonfiction and his life's work. His storytelling gifts tap into humankind's collective psyche in the most inspiring and reassuring ways. His grail quest gives hope to an ailing planet and its inhabitants, including nonhuman entities. Without meaning to embarrass him, aficionados and scholars might suggest "it's all one water," that Barry Lopez is just as likely to be awarded the Nobel Peace Prize as the Nobel Prize in Literature.

Acknowledgments

No Bottom could not have emerged without the usual struggles and serendipitous events classic to all heartfelt journeys. Since the mid-'80s, Patrick Meanor knew of my enthusiasm for Barry Lopez's works. Upon bumping into Pat while coming out of a movie house in April 1999, he invited me to write a lit-bio article on Barry's short stories, for a popular literary series he was editing. I embraced the project wholeheartedly and have since traveled, read, researched and written relentlessly.

Barry's open and unequivocal responses to the blizzard of literary/biographical questions I posed in correspondence fueled a deep, abiding respect for the man behind the work. His generosity of spirit is the signature style of an extraordinary person. His behaviors manifest the voices of Ishmael, Wallace Stegner and Wendell Berry (among others) who infused Barry with ideals of companionship, personal responsibility and community.

Creative differences with the senior editor of the lit-bio series eventually caused my withdrawal of the article. Ironically, it also prompted a wellspring of dialogues with Jerry Kelly, a dear friend from the mid-'70s who is a fellow writer and a small press publisher. Jerry insisted on publishing the lit-bio in book form. Since 2004, we have collaborated on design, format and content. His resourcefulness, succinct editing suggestions and unwavering belief in the project have generated conceptual catalysts that morphed ambiguous intent.

Elsewhere, in response to a plea for macrophotos of the Pacific Madrone, my effervescent daughter, Sara Beth, effortlessly located several on-line. Our good friend and neighbor, Helen Stayman, provocatively nudged me with an indispensible array of incisive editing comments, for which I am beholden. My lovely wife, Phyllis, remains resolute in her support and devotion, without which I would be bereft of this orb's most fundamental quest.

Source Notes

Abbreviations Used for Sources

ASR Audio and Sound Recordings
B Books
ES Electronic Sources
I Interview in *No Bottom*
("Conversations with Barry Lopez," 17–58)
JNA Journal and Newspaper Articles
UM Unpublished Material

Page

viii *"The way we take"*: **JNA**, Ryan, *Higher (Literary) Elevations*, 3.

FOREWORD

xii *the Pacific madrone*: **B**, National Audubon, *"Pacific Madrone,"* 577–578.

xiv *"I find my name"*: **UM**, Lopez and Newell, Correspondence, September 11, 2002.

xv *one that is unique*: **UM**, Lopez and Newell, Correspondence, August 9, 2007.

PHOTOGRAPHS

60 *"the Three Sisters"*: **UM**, Lopez and Newell, Correspondence, December 28, 2007.

62 *"Two views of the bridge"*: **UM**, Lopez and Newell, Correspondence, December 28, 2007.

63 *…and from the water line*: **UM**, Lopez and Newell, Correspondence, December 28, 2007.

A CRITICAL DISCUSSION: THE SHORT STORY BOOKS
INTRODUCTION

67 *"You use non-autobiographical"*: **I**, See 20 ("Conversations with Barry Lopez").

67 *"Early on, I"*: **I**, See 30 ("Conversations with Barry Lopez").

67 *"It is by such early"*: **B**, Lopez, *Winter Count*, "Tapestry," 69.

68 *"reinforce in us"*: **I**, See 37 ("Conversations with Barry Lopez").

THE FORMATIVE YEARS

69 *"some of Lopez's"*: **B**, Elder, *American Nature*, "Barry Lopez," 549.

70 *written when he*: **JNA**, Warner, *Northwest*, "Annotated Bibliography," 137.

70 *"instrument of grace"*: **B**, Elder, *American Nature*, "Barry Lopez," 550.

70 *"lasted almost thirty"*: **JNA**, Tydeman, *Northwest*, "Interview with Barry Lopez," 109.

71 *"did not separate humanity"*: **JNA**, O'Connell, *"On Sacred Ground,"* 60.

71 *"loved the irreverence"*: **I**, See 21 ("Conversations with Barry Lopez").

Page

71   *Lopez's literary apprenticeship:* **JNA**, Warner, *Northwest*, "Annotated Bibliography,"
      117-137.

A Literary Preamble

72   *"traditional Tsanchifin" / "Cascade Physiographic":* **UM**, Lopez and Newell,
      Correspondence, July 2, 2007.

72   *"the impulse to write":* **I**, See 36 ("Conversations with Barry Lopez").

72   *"as the writers of another generation":* **ES**, Lopez, *"Literature of Place."*

72   *"led with moral":* **ES**, Calypso Consulting, *"Interview with Barry Lopez,"* 2.

73   *"sounds common to the region":* **JNA**, Western American Literature, "Interview,"
      16.

73   *"You're the storyteller":* **I**, See 44 ("Conversations with Barry Lopez").

73   *"the security of the familiar":* **JNA**, Shapiro, "Against the Current," 6.

73   *"to ground the reader":* **JNA**, Shapiro, "Against the Current," 6.

73   *"honor the unspoken":* **B**, Lopez, *Field Notes,* "Wiideema," 102.

73   *"the idea of darkness":* **JNA**, Warner, *Northwest*, "Annotated Bibliography," 131.

73   *"reader's companion, [rather]":* **I**, See 44 ("Conversations with Barry Lopez").

74   *"to construct something":* **ES**, Mordue, *"Conversation with Barry Lopez,"* 6.

74   *"to formalize the relationship":* **JNA**, O'Connell, *Sierra*, "On Sacred Ground," 60.

74   *"a spiritual teaching":* **B**, Aveling, *Jesuits*, "Ignatius Loyola's Early Life," 52.

74   *"these other epistemologies" / "as rigorous and valid":* **ES**, Lopez, *Resurgence 192*,
      "Language of Animals," 2.

76   *metaphorical, nonthreatening and:* **B**, Bettelheim, *Uses*, "Introduction," 12-19.

76   *"the only safe containers":* **B**, Lopez, *Field Notes*, "Wiideema," 98.

77   *"You will think you":* **B**, Lopez, *Desert Notes*, "Desert," 4.

77   *"a writer who travels":* **ES**, Carnegie, *Three Rivers Lecture Series*,
      http://www.clpgh.org/exhibit/neighborhoods/oakland/oak_centv.html.

77   *"was one of three finalists":* **ES**, Lopez, *Official Website*, "Recent Work."

79   *"to underscore the need":* **JNA**, Lopez, *Northwest*, "Interview," 110.

79   *"genius of community":* **JNA**, Martin, *Georgia Review*, "On Resistance," 18.

80   *"in the fabric of":* **ES**, Lopez, *Official Website*, "Gallery."

80   *"The way we take care":* **JNA**, Ryan, *Higher (Literary) Elevations*, 3.

80   *an environy that occurred when:* **JNA**, Lopez, *Northwest*, "Interview," 114-115.

80   *"an important arena":* **JNA**, Tydeman, *Northwest Review*, "Interview," 104.

80   *"always wanted to do":* **JNA**, Tydeman, *Northwest Review*, "Interview," 115.

81   *"blueprints for the imagination":* **JNA**, Shapiro, "Against the Current," 12.

81   *"in the world of comparative":* **JNA**, Shapiro, "Against the Current," 9.

81   *One of the marvelous things:* **B**, Lueders, *Writing Natural History*, 16.

Desert Notes: Reflections in the Eye of a Raven

81   *"probably":* **I**, See 21 ("Conversations with Barry Lopez").

81   *"This is the way":* **I**, See 22 ("Conversations with Barry Lopez").

82   *"through a series of":* **B**, Lopez, *Desert Notes*, "Introduction," xiii.

82   *"that we must get all":* **B**, Lopez, *Desert Notes*, "Desert," 3.

Page

82   *"take things down"*: **B**, Lopez, *Desert Notes*, "Desert," 4.
83   *"a golden eagle sitting"*: **B**, Lopez, *Desert Notes*, "Hot," 11.
83   *"careful with the silence"*: **B**, Lopez, *Desert Notes*, "Hot," 11.
83   *"the sulphurous fumes"*: **B**, Lopez, *Desert Notes*, "Hot," 11.
83   *"the pressure of his"*: **B**, Lopez, *Desert Notes*, "Hot," 13.
83   *"never again hear a map"*: **B**, Lopez, *Desert Notes*, "Directions," 87.
83   *"famous desert"*: **B**, Lopez, *Desert Notes*, "Directions," 86.
84   *"fooled by ravens"*: **JNA**, Lopez, *American West*, "Ravens," 40–41.
84   *"to grasp and hold fast"*: **B**, Lopez, *Desert Notes*, "Raven," 22.
85   *"like a boulder fallen"*: **B**, Lopez, *Desert Notes*, "Coyote," 81.
85   *"trapped inside the flowers"*: **B**, Lopez, *Desert Notes*, "Coyote," 81.
85   *"something could not come"*: **B**, Lopez, *Desert Notes*, "Coyote," 79.
85   *"try and clean it out"*: **B**, Lopez, *Desert Notes*, "School," 66.
85   *"two hundred miles"*: **B**, Lopez, *Desert Notes*, "School," 66.
85   *"establish some sense"*: **B**, Lueders, *Writing Natural History*, 33.
86   *"all died within"*: **B**, Lopez, *Desert Notes*, "Blue," 47.
86   *"a series of blue"*: **B**, Lopez, *Desert Notes*, "Blue," 48.
86   *"a hard, white stone"*: **B**, Lopez, *Desert Notes*, "Blue," 48.
86   *"have been shifting"*: **B**, Lopez, *Desert Notes*, "Blue," 51.
86   *"to become the companion"*: **ES**, Lopez, *"Literature of Place."*
86   *"an impulse to write out"*: **I**, See 24 ("Conversations with Barry Lopez").
86   *"you wait for yourself"*: **B**, Lopez, *Desert Notes*, "Conversation," 55.
86   *"sunlight will bounce"*: **B**, Lopez, *Desert Notes*, "Conversation," 57.

River Notes: The Dance of Herons

88   *"a landscape of facts"*: **I**, See 19 ("Conversations with Barry Lopez").
88   *"Desert Notes is playful"*: **I**, See 21 ("Conversations with Barry Lopez").
88   *"a sound that would"*: **B**, Lopez, *River Notes*, "Introduction," x.
88   *"her small teakwood trunk"*: **B**, Lopez, *River Notes*, "Introduction," xii.
89   *"loss of guile"*: **B**, Lopez, *River Notes*, "Introduction," xiii.
89   *"when your fingers brush"*: **B**, Lopez, *River Notes*, "Introduction," xiii.
89   *"to cry out or shriek"*: **B**, Martin, *Folklore*, 88.
89   *"expect the wisdom"*: **B**, Lopez, *River Notes*, "Search," 5.
89   *"bits of bone from fish"*: **B**, Lopez, *River Notes*, "Search," 8.
89   *"a great dream"*: **B**, Lopez, *River Notes*, "Search," 8.
90   *"an unpronounceable forgiveness"*: **B**, Lopez, *River Notes*, "Search," 9.
90   *"begin to appear"*: **B**, Lopez, *River Notes*, "Search," 9.
90   *"a big tree barberchairing"*: **B**, Lopez, *River Notes*, "Log," 13.
90   *"lived as well as could be"*: **B**, Lopez, *River Notes*, "Log," 23.
91   *"it's easiest to live"*: **B**, Lopez, *River Notes*, "Rapids," 54.
91   *"an elegant series"*: **B**, Lopez, *River Notes*, "Bend," 29.
91   *"to feel, raccoonlike"*: **B**, Lopez, *River Notes*, "Bend," 30.
91   *"look[s] up in perfect silence"*: **B**, Custer, *Adventures*, "When I Heard the Learn'd Astronomer," 49.

Page

91   *"dismantled my loneliness"*: **B**, Lopez, *River Notes,* "Bend," 31.

92   *"only commentary on the river's"*: **B**, Lopez, *River Notes,* "Drought," 95.

92   *"as one visits those dying"*: **B**, Lopez, *River Notes,* "Drought," 96.

92   *"a loss of conviction"*: **B**, Lopez, *River Notes,* "Drought," 98.

92   *"remembers how to live"*: **B**, Lopez, *River Notes,* "Drought," 99.

92   *"Everyone has to learn"*: **B**, Lopez, *River Notes,* "Drought," 100.

92   *"the earth together in"*: **B**, Lopez, *River Notes,* "Drought," 100.

92   *"wisdom of the desert"*: **B**, Lopez, *River Notes,* "Search," 5.

92   *"of things so beautiful"*: **ES**, Lopez, *Nature Writing,* "Introduction," 3.

93   *"an artist in language"*: **B**, Lopez, *River Notes,* Dustjacket/Edward Abbey.

93   *"his work had the fascination"*: **B**, Lopez, *River Notes,* Dustjacket/Diane Wakoski.

Winter Count

93   *"pictographically on a buffalo"*: **B**, Lopez, *Winter Count,* from author's note (untitled and page not numbered) preceding "Restoration."

93   *"as if on a prairie"*: **B**, Lopez, *Winter Count,* "Winter," 24.

94   *"proof against some undefined"*: **B**, Lopez, *Winter Count,* "Woman," 81.

94   *"honor the unspoken request"*: **B**, Lopez, *Field Notes,* "Wiideema," 102.

94   *"accurate and sympathetic"*: **B**, Lopez, *Winter Count,* "Restoration," 8.

95   *"beveled a frayed corner"*: **B**, Lopez, *Winter Count,* "Restoration," 6.

95   *"a new understanding"*: **B**, Lopez, *Winter Count,* "Restoration," 9.

95   *"owners of the landscape"*: **B**, Lopez, *Winter Count,* "Restoration," 12.

95   *"the individual view"*: **B**, Lopez, *Winter Count,* "Winter," 61.

96   *"a beaded bag of white"*: **B**, Lopez, *Winter Count,* "Winter," 55.

96   *"only tell the story"*: **B**, Lopez, *Winter Count,* "Winter," 61.

96   *"thrown away everything"*: **B**, Lopez, *Winter Count,* "Winter," 59.

96   *"proving you are right"*: **B**, Lopez, *Winter Count,* "Winter," 59.

96   *"all that is holding"*: **B**, Lopez, *Winter Count,* "Winter," 62.

96   *"barking-dog sounds of geese"*: **B**, Lopez, *Winter Count,* "Winter," 63.

97   *"they fell victim to"*: **B**, Lopez, *Winter Count,* "Location," 109.

97   *"a sort of willful irritation"*: **B**, Lopez, *Winter Count,* "Location," 102.

97   *"in the shapes of"*: **B**, Lopez, *Winter Count,* "Location," 105.

97   *"ritual cleansing and dreaming"*: **B**, Lopez, *Winter Count,* "Location," 110.

97   *"learning everything wrong"*: **B**, Lopez, *Winter Count,* "Location," 111.

97   *"an impossible task"*: **B**, Lopez, *Winter Count,* "Orrery," 42.

98   *"there is probably nothing that cannot"*: **B**, Lopez, *Winter Count,* "Orrery," 49.

98   *"scenes of rustic"*: **B**, Lopez, *Winter Count,* "Tapestry," 70.

98   *"of some catastrophe"*: **B**, Lopez, *Winter Count,* "Tapestry," 71.

98   *"go on doing whatever"*: **B**, Lopez, *Winter Count,* "Tapestry," 72.

98   *"rid of a daunting"*: **B**, Lopez, *Winter Count,* "Tapestry," 75.

98   *"cranelike movements"*: **B**, Lopez, *Winter Count,* "Woman," 80.

98   *"seen before only in the"*: **B**, Lopez, *Winter Count,* "Woman," 81.

98   *"Mikado yellow, cerulean blue"*: **B**, Lopez, *Winter Count,* "Woman," 84.

Page

98   *"delicately tinged"*: **B**, Lopez, *Winter Count*, "Woman," 85.
98   *"patterns like African fabric"*: **B**, Lopez, *Winter Count*, "Woman," 85.
99   *"imagined it was possible"*: **B**, Lopez, *Winter Count*, "Woman," 86.
99   *"barrio of East Los Angeles"*: **B**, Lopez, *Winter Count*, "Lover," 89.
99   *"understood how words healed"*: **B**, Lopez, *Winter Count*, "Lover," 89.
99   *"between ideas and work"*: **B**, Lopez, *Winter Count*, "Lover," 92.
99   *"the sight of his hard"*: **B**, Lopez, *Winter Count*, "Lover," 97.
99   *"of the inscrutable life"*: **B**, Lopez, *Winter Count*, "Lover," 97.
99   *"other bends in the river"*: **B**, Lopez, *Winter Count*, "Lover," 97.
100   *"impenetrable privacy"*: **B**, Lopez, *Winter Count*, "Lover," 96.
100   *"quiet desperation"*: **B**, *21st Century*, Princeton Language Institute, 122.
100   *"radiant with possibilities"*: **B**, Lopez, *Winter Count*, Dustjacket/William Kittredge.

Field Notes: The Grace Note of the Canyon Wren

101   *"an indicator of where"*: **I**, See 22 ("Conversations with Barry Lopez").
101   *"human dignity and the nature"*: **ES**, Calypso Consulting, *"Interview with Barry Lopez,"* 2.
103   *"the unceasing kindness"*: **B**, Lopez, *Field Notes*, "Introduction," 5.
103   *"they loved, that they"*: **B**, Lopez, *Field Notes*, "Introduction," 8.
103   *"[h]eadwaters of the Oso"*: **B**, Lopez, *Field Notes*, "Introduction," 11.
103   *"the running tide"*: **B**, Lopez, *Field Notes*, "Introduction," 11.
103   *"kept the world from"*: **B**, Lopez, *Field Notes*, "Teal," 21.
103   *"disarming morality"*: **B**, Lopez, *Field Notes*, "Teal," 21.
103   *"feel as if nothing"*: **B**, Lopez, *Field Notes*, "Teal," 23.
103   *"grandfather's stories of Ohio"*: **B**, Lopez, *Field Notes*, "Empira's," 27.
104   *"committed to memory"*: **B**, Lopez, *Field Notes*, "Empira's," 27.
104   *"in a different way"*: **B**, Lopez, *Field Notes*, "Entreaty," 99.
104   *"disturb these people"*: **B**, Lopez, *Field Notes*, "Entreaty," 91.
104   *"menacing curiosity"*: **B**, Lopez, *Field Notes*, "Entreaty," 97.
105   *"its two minute slabs"*: **B**, Lopez, *Field Notes*, "Entreaty," 94.
105   *"the way a bird"*: **B**, Lopez, *Field Notes*, "Entreaty," 96.
105   *"companionship with the Wiideema"*: **B**, Lopez, *Field Notes*, "Entreaty," 100.
105   *"to understand now"*: **B**, Lopez, *Field Notes*, "Entreaty," 102.
105   *"to travel intimately across"*: **B**, Lopez, *Field Notes*, "Negro," 83.
105   *"put on another cup"*: **B**, Lopez, *Field Notes*, "Negro," 88.
105   *"the evolutionary biology"*: **B**, Lopez, *Field Notes*, "Homecoming," 105.
106   *"by their shadows"*: **B**, Lopez, *Field Notes*, "Homecoming," 111.
106   *"Only when that gift"*: **B**, Lopez, *Field Notes*, "Pearyland," 71.
106   *"to be near animals"*: **B**, Lopez, *Field Notes*, "Lessons," 137.
106   *"a kind of love"*: **JNA**, O'Connell, *Sierra*, "On Sacred Ground," 81.
106   *"saw no greater purpose"*: **B**, Lopez, *Field Notes*, "Open," 40.
107   *"church bells buried"*: **B**, Lopez, *Field Notes*, "Sonora," 117.
107   *"given herself away"*: **B**, Lopez, *Field Notes*, "Runner," 157.

Light Action in the Caribbean

Page

109   *"perhaps from Venezuela"*: **B**, Lopez, *Light Action*, "Mornings," 99.

109   *"telling of beautiful untrue"*: **B**, Wilde, *Complete Works*, "Decay of Lying," 970-992.

110   *"a stray bullet one night"*: **B**, Lopez, *Light Action*, "Deaf," 64.

111   *"until he makes a mess"*: **B**, Lopez, *Light Action*, "Deaf," 66.

111   *"waving big money around"*: **B**, Lopez, *Light Action*, "Stolen," 12.

111   *"on these three-hundred-acre"*: **B**, Lopez, *Light Action*, "Stolen," 11.

111   *"ranched that central"*: **B**, Lopez, *Light Action*, "Stolen," 12.

111   *"even literally which way"*: **B**, Lopez, *Light Action*, "Stolen," 12.

112   *"in the starlight"*: **B**, Lopez, *Light Action*, "Stolen," 13.

112   *"in command of"*: **B**, Lopez, *Light Action*, "Light," 128.

113   *"Put dem over"*: **B**, Lopez, *Light Action*, "Light," 139.

113   *"the counsel of [their]"*: **B**, Lopez, *Light Action*, "Emory," 47.

114   *"along the Marias River"*: **B**, Lopez, *Light Action*, "Emory," 49.

114   *"sleep in my hands"*: **B**, Lopez, *Light Action*, "Remembering," 9.

114   *"long pants and travel[s]"*: **B**, Lopez, *Light Action*, "Mornings," 104.

114   *"birds and sand dunes"*: **B**, Lopez, *Light Action*, "Mornings," 102.

114   *"reactionary fanatics who rigged"*: **B**, Lopez, *Light Action*, "Mornings," 104.

115   *"a spiritual revolution"*: **B**, Lopez, *Light Action*, "Letters," 89.

115   *"their humanity, the fearless"*: **B**, Lopez, *Light Action*, "Letters," 88.

115   *"intensified rather than quenched"*: **B**, Lopez, *Light Action*, "Letters," 88.

115   *"the Spanish viceroyalty"* / *"a period of"*: **B**, Lopez, *Light Action*, "Letters," 90.

115   *"off the ground before"*: **B**, Lopez, *Light Action*, "Letters," 90.

115   *"square-rigged, three-masted ship"*: **B**, Lopez, *Light Action*, "Construction," 116.

115   *"were adaptable and willing"*: **B**, Lopez, *Light Action*, "Construction," 124.

116   *"starved, angered and humiliated"*: **B**, Lopez, *Light Action*, "Lords," 38.

116   *"of the place from"*: **B**, Lopez, *Light Action*, "Mappist," 152.

116   *"shows history and how"*: **B**, Lopez, *Light Action*, "Mappist," 159.

116   *"the venality of material"*: **B**, Lopez, *Light Action*, "Mappist," 160.

116   *"to discover the kind of"*: **B**, Lopez, *Light Action*, "Mappist," 160.

117   *"tough-minded, emotionally turbulent"*: **B**, Lopez, *Light Action*, Dustjacket/Russell Banks.

117   *"is full of delicate"*: **JNA**, Draper, *New York Times*, "Doing What Comes."

Resistance

117   *"admiration for their politics"*: **JNA**, Martin, *Georgia Review*, "On Resistance," 16.

118   *"since the Florida"*: **JNA**, Martin, *Georgia Review*, "On Resistance," 25.

118   *"that community, not the"*: **ES**, Lopez, *Official Website*, "News/Photos."

118   *"to get the setup first"*: **JNA**, Martin, *Georgia Review*, "On Resistance," 28.

119   *"writers, artists and scholars"*: **ES**, Lopez, *Official Website*, "Home."

119   *"Investigator of Moral"*: **B**, Bradbury, *Martian*, "Usher II," 191-211.

119   *"a repressive United States"*: **ES**, Lopez, *Official Website*, "Home."

119   *"proportion in life"*: **B**, Lopez, *Resistance*, "Apocalypse," 11.

Page

119   *"an appetite for distraction"*: **B**, Lopez, *Resistance*, "Apocalypse," 11.

119   *"people who celebrate"*: **B**, Lopez, *Resistance*, "Apocalypse," 7.

119   *"what endures is simple devotion"*: **B**, Lopez, *Resistance*, "Apocalypse," 4.

119   *"the histories of other"*: **B**, Lopez, *Resistance*, "Apocalypse," 9.

119   *"by tides we don't"*: **B**, Lopez, *Resistance*; "Apocalypse," 5.

120   *"love what Owen Daniels"*: **JNA**, Martin, *Georgia Review*, "On Resistance," 30.

120   *"quiet elucidation of those"*: **JNA**, Martin, *Georgia Review*, "On Resistance," 30.

120   *"the histories of other"*: **B**, Lopez, *Resistance*, "Apocalypse," 9.

120   *"lead lives of quiet"*: **B**, *21st Century*, Princeton Language Institute, 122.

120   *"dismantled [his] loneliness"*: **B**, Lopez, *River Notes*, "Bend," 31.

121   *"practical things"*: **B**, Lopez, *Resistance*, "Bear," 76.

121   *"alone for four days"*: **B**, Lopez, *Resistance*, "Bear," 76.

121   *"father's scorn for ideas"*: **B**, Lopez, *Resistance*, "Bear," 75.

121   *"would not give in to"*: **B**, Lopez, *Resistance*, "Bear," 81.

121   *"the rustling and voices of"*: **B**, Lopez, *Resistance*, "Bear," 81.

121   *"same camp above the"*: **B**, Lopez, *Resistance*, "Bear," 88.

121   *"how one small thing"*: **B**, Lopez, *Resistance*, "Bear," 74.

121   *"pay attention"*: **B**, Lopez, *Resistance*, "Bear," 78.

121   *"everything, even the buffalo"*: **B**, Lopez, *Resistance*, "Bear," 86.

121   *"you have to keep"*: **B**, Lopez, *Resistance*, "Bear," 86.

121   *"how [the land] had"*: **B**, Lopez, *Resistance*, "Bear," 73.

121   *"seeing some young woman"*: **B**, Lopez, *Resistance*, "Bear," 85.

122   *"Porcupine Creek"*: **B**, Lopez, *Resistance*, "Bear," 76, 72, 77, 74, 79.

122   *"God-given right"*: **B**, Lopez, *Resistance*, "Bear," 78.

122   *as expressed in Roderick*: **B**, Nash, *Wilderness*, "Wilderness Condition," 33-43.

122   *"all one's efforts are"*: **B**, Lopez, *Resistance*, "Nílch'i," 140.

122   *"human social arrangements"*: **B**, Lopez, *Resistance*, "Nílch'i," 133.

122   *"Navajo belief [that] winds"*: **B**, Lopez, *Resistance*, "Nílch'i," 138.

122   *"the longest-known and most"*: **B**, Lopez, *Resistance*, "Nílch'i," 140.

122   *"leave no trace of"*: **B**, Lopez, *Resistance*, "Nílch'i," 127.

123   *"flow beautifully over"*: **B**, Lopez, *Field Notes*, "Negro," 83.

123   *"looked across the desert"*: **B**, Lopez, *Desert Notes*, "Hot," 13.

123   *"desire for unbounded"*: **B**, Lopez, *Resistance*, "Walls," 92.

123   *"Urumchi street slang"*: **B**, Lopez, *Resistance*, "Walls," 97.

123   *"a book of landscape"*: **B**, Lopez, *Resistance*, "Walls," 102.

123   *"original evidence for"*: **B**, Lopez, *Resistance*, "Walls," 93.

124   *"to be vigilant and"*: **JNA**, Martin, *Georgia Review*, "On Resistance," 28.

124   *"theologies of creation"*: **B**, Lopez, *Resistance*, "Nílch'i," 128.

124   *"other, older cultures"*: **B**, Lopez, *Resistance*, "Apocalypse," 9.

124   *"something crucial in [her]"*: **B**, Lopez, *Resistance*, "Rio de la Plata," 29.

124   *"in Bergen-Belsen"*: **B**, Lopez, *Resistance*, "Rio de la Plata," 33.

124   *"triumph and despair"*: **B**, Lopez, *Resistance*, "Rio de la Plata," 33.

125   *"at rich men's tables"*: **B**, Emerson, *Collected*, "Forbearance," 67.

Page

125 *"a kind of instruction"* / *"for whom harm"*: **B**, Lopez, *Resistance*, "Mortise," 40.

125 *"salvaged teak wood"*: **B**, Lopez, *Resistance*, "Mortise," 50.

125 *"lived near Abashiri"*: **B**, Lopez, *Resistance*, "Mortise," 51.

125 *"to wash out the anger"*: **B**, Lopez, *Resistance*, "Traveling," 68.

125 *"summer juice running down"*: **B**, Lopez, *Resistance*, "Traveling," 68.

125 *"not be [among] the martyred"*: **B**, Baudelaire, *Twenty*, 46.

126 *"to be vigilant"*: **B**, Lopez, *Resistance*, "Traveling," 59.

126 *"the forbidden pleasure"*: **B**, Lopez, *Resistance*, "Traveling," 65.

126 *"the geographic cure"*: **B**, Lopez, *Resistance*, "Flight," 153.

126 *"other, older cultures"*: **B**, Lopez, *Resistance*, "Apocalypse," 9.

126 *"of dengue hemorrhagic fever"*: **B**, Lopez, *Resistance*, "Flight," 154.

126 *"how to live 'quietly'"*: **B**, Lopez, *Resistance*, "Flight," 146.

126 *"putting the face to"*: **B**, Lopez, *Resistance*, "Flight," 145.

126 *"drawing by dialogue"*: **B**, Lopez, *Resistance*, "Flight," 147.

126 *"been restored"*: **B**, Lopez, *Resistance*, "Flight," 143.

126 *"became a docent in a"*: **B**, Lopez, *Resistance*, "Flight," 156.

126 *"to be vigilant, or"*: **B**, Lopez, *Resistance*, "Flight," 156.

127 *"¡Nunca Màs!"*: **B**, Lopez, *Resistance,* "Flight," 157.

127 *"30,000 killed"*: **B**, Argentine National Commission, *¡Nunca Màs!*.

127 *"the question of genocide"*: **B**, Lopez, *¡Nunca Màs!*, 9.

127 *"socially responsible literature"*: **ES**, Bellwether Prize, *In Support of a Literature of Social Change*, "Defining a literature of social change," http://www.bellwether-prize.org/change.html.

127 *"a social impulse"*: **I**, See 36 ("Conversations with Barry Lopez").

127 *"now, an artistic vision that"*: **JNA**, Martin, *Georgia Review*, "On Resistance," 15.

127 *"true believers"*: **B**, Hoffer, *True Believer*.

127 *"careful not to declare any"*: **B**, Lopez, *Resistance*, "Flight," 157.

127 *"a work of luminous"* / *"are daring, sensuous"*: **B**, Lopez, *Resistance*, Dustjacket/Jim Crace.

EPILOGUE

133 *"it's all one water"*: **B**, Lopez, *Resistance*, "Flight," 145.

Bibliography

Books

Argentine National Commission on Disappeared. *Nunca Más: The Report of the Argentine National Commission on the Disappeared.* October 1986.

Armstrong, Edward A. *The Life and Lore of the Bird: In Nature, Art, Myth, and Literature.* New York: Crown Publishers, 1975.

————. *The Wren.* Shire Natural History 59. Buckinghamshire, UK: Shire Publications, 1992.

Aveling, J. C. H. *The Jesuits.* New York: Dorset Press, 1987.

Baudelaire, Charles. *Twenty Prose Poems.* Translated from the French *Petits Poèmes en Prose* by Michael Hamburger. London: Jonathan Cape, Ltd., 1968.

Bettelheim, Bruno. *The Uses of Enchantment: The Meaning and Importance of Fairy Tales.* New York: Vintage Books, 1989.

Black Elk. *Black Elk Speaks.* New York: Pocket Books, 1973.

Bradbury, Ray. *Fahrenheit 451.* New York: Simon and Schuster, 1967.

————. *The Martian Chronicles.* Norwalk, Ct: The Heritage Press, Inc. 1974.

Campbell, Joseph. *The Hero with a Thousand Faces.* Princeton, N.J.: Princeton University Press, 1968.

Clavell, James. *Whirlwind.* New York: William Morrow, 1986.

Custer, Edwin C. *Adventures in Poetry.* New York: Harcourt Brace Jovanovich, Inc. 1964.

Dictionary of World Myth: An A-Z Reference Guide to Gods, Goddesses, Heroes, Heroines and Fabulous Beasts. General Consultant: Roy Willis. London: Duncan Baird, 1995.

Elder, John, Ed. *American Nature Writers I.* New York: Charles Scribner's Sons, 1996. 549-568.

Emerson, Ralph Waldo. *Collected Poems and Translations.* New York: Library of America, 1994.

Forey, Pamela, and Cecilia Fitzsimons. *An Instant Guide to Seashells: The Most Familiar Species of North American Seashells Described and Illustrated in Full Color.* New York: Gramercy Books, 2000.

Harrison, Hal H. *American Birds in Color: Land Birds.* New York: Wm. H. Wise & Co., 1951.

Hay, John. *In Defense of Nature.* Iowa City, IA: University of Iowa Press, 1969.

Herzberg, Max J. *Myths and Their Meaning.* Boston: Allyn and Bacon, 1984.

Hoffer, Eric. *The True Believer: Thoughts on the Nature of Mass Movements.* New York: Harper & Brothers, 1951.

Ignatius of Loyola, Saint. *The Spiritual Exercises of St. Ignatius.* Translated by Thomas Corbishley. New York: P.J. Kenedy, 1963.

London, Jack. The Iron Heel. New York: Grosset & Dunlap, 1907.

Lopez, Barry. *About This Life: Journeys on the Threshold of Memory.* New York: Alfred A. Knopf, 1998.

————. *Apologia.* Woodcuts by Robin Eschner. Athens, GA: University of Georgia Press, 1998.

————. *Arctic Dreams: Imagination and Desire in a Northern Landscape.* New York: Charles Scribner's Sons, 1986.

————. *Crow and Weasel.* Illustrations by Tom Pohrt. San Francisco: North Point Press, 1990.

————. *Desert Notes: Reflections in the Eye of a Raven.* Kansas City: Sheed, Andrews & McMeel, 1976.

————. *Field Notes: The Grace Note of the Canyon Wren.* New York: Alfred A. Knopf, 1995.

————. *Giving Birth to Thunder, Sleeping with His Daughter: Coyote Builds North America.* New York: Avon Books, 1990.

————, ed. *Home Ground: Language for an American Landscape.* Managing ed.: Debra Gwartney. San Antonio: Trinity University Press, 2006.

————. *Lessons from the Wolverine.* Illustrations by Tom Pohrt. Athens, GA: University of Georgia Press, 1997.

————. *Light Action in the Caribbean: Stories.* New York: Alfred A. Knopf, 2000.

————. *¡Nunca Màs!* Red Wing, MN: Red Dragonfly Press, 2007.

————. *Of Wolves and Men.* New York: Charles Scribner's Sons, 1978.

————. *The Rediscovery of North America.* Lexington, KY: University Press of Kentucky, 1990.

————. *Resistance.* New York: Alfred A. Knopf, 2004.

————. *River Notes: The Dance of Herons.* Kansas City: Andrews and McMeel, 1979.

————. *Winter Count.* New York: Charles Scribner's Sons, 1981.

Lopez, Ken. *Nature Writing: A Catalog.* Hadley, Mass: K. Lopez, 2000.

Lueders, Edward. *Writing Natural History: Dialogues with Authors.* Salt Lake City: University of Utah Press, 1989.

Martin, Laura C. *The Folklore of Birds.* Illustrations by Mauro Magellan. Old Saybrook, CT: Globe Pequot Press, 1993.

National Audubon Society Field Guide to North American Trees: Western Region. New York: Alfred A. Knopf, 2000.

Nash, Roderick. *Wilderness and the American Mind.* 3rd ed. New Haven, CT: Yale University Press, 1982.

O'Connell, Nicholas. *At the Field's End: Interviews with Twenty Pacific Northwest Writers.* Seattle: Madrona, 1987.

———. *On Sacred Ground: The Spirit of Place in Pacific Northwest Literature.* Seattle: Washington University Press, 2003.

———. "Barry Lopez." In *At the Field's End: Interviews with Twenty Pacific Northwest Writers.* 3-18. Seattle: Madrona, 1987.

Payne, Daniel G. "Barry Lopez." In *Dictionary of Literary Biography: American Short-Story Writers Since WWII.* 335. Edited by Richard E. Lee and Patrick Meanor. 187-97. Farmington Hills, MI: Thomson Gale, 2007.

Peterson, Roger Tory. *Peterson First Guide to Birds of North America.* Boston: Houghton Mifflin, 1986.

Proctor, Noble. *Songbirds: How to Attract Them and Identify Their Songs.* Emmaus, PA: Rodale Press,1988.

Sherman, Paul. *For Love of the World: Essays on Nature Writers.* "Making the Turn: Rereading Barry Lopez." Iowa City: University of Iowa Press, 1992.

Slovic, Scott. *Seeking Awareness in American Nature Writing: Henry Thoreau, Annie Dillard, Edward Abbey, Wendell Berry, Barry Lopez.* Salt Lake City: University of Utah Press, 1992, 137-166.

Stewart, Frank, and Barry Lopez, eds. *Maps of Reconciliation: Literature and the Ethical Imagination.* Manoa 19:2. Honolulu: University of Hawai'i Press, 2007.

Stickney, Eleanor H. *A Little Bird Told Me So: Birds in Mythology and History.* Danbury, CT: Rutledge Books, 1997.

21st Century Dictionary of Quotations. Ed. by Princeton Language Institute. New York: Laurel, 1993.

Wild, Peter. *Barry Lopez.* Western Writers Series, no. 64. Boise, Idaho: Boise State University, 1984.

Wilde, Oscar. *Complete Works of Oscar Wilde.* London: Collins, 1966.

Wilson, Edward O. *The Creation.* New York: W. W. Norton & Company, Inc., 2006.

Zamyatin, Yevgeny. *We.* Translation by Mirra Ginsburg. New York: EOS, 1999.

Zaleski, Philip, Ed. *Best Spiritual Writing 1999.* "The Language of

Animals." San Francisco, CA: Harper San Francisco 1999. 174-183.

Journal and Newspaper Articles

Abood, Maureen. "God Between the Lines." *U.S. Catholic, 63,* June 1998: 22-23.

Aton, Jim. "An Interview with Barry Lopez." *Western American Literature, 21.* May 1986.

Bonetti, Kay. "An Interview with Barry Lopez." *Missouri Review* 11, no. 3 (1988): 59-77.

Evans, Alice. "Leaning Into the Light: An Interview with Barry Lopez." *Poets and Writers* 22 (March/April 1994): 62-79.

Hellman, David. "Lopez, Barry: Resistance." *Library Journal,* June 15, 2004, 59.

Lopez, Barry. "A Literature of Place." *Heat 2,* 1966: 52-58.

———. "A Quiet Voice in the Wilderness." *U.S. Catholic,* Dec. 1973: 30-32.

———. "Benjamin Claire, North Dakota Tradesman, Writes to the President of the United States." *North American Review,* Sept.-Oct. 1992: 16-20.

———. "Cold Scapes." Photographs by Bernhard Edmaier. *National Geographic* 212, no. 6 (December 2007):136-55.

———. "My Horse." *North American Review,* Summer 1975: 8-10.

———. "The Gift." *Ave Maria,* Mar. 19, 1966: 22-23.

———. "Ravens." American West, Jan.-Feb. 1984: 80-81.

———. "The Himalayan Parchment." *Brick* [Canada], Fall 2000: 153-156.

———. "The Interior of North Dakota." *Paris Review,* Winter 1992: 134-144.

———. "The Language of Animals." *Wild Earth,* Summer 1998: inside front cover, 2-6.

———. "The Passing of the Night." Audubon, July 1975: 18-25.

———. "Waiting for Salmon." *The Sun,* no. 366: 13-17.

———. "Writer, Storyteller, Healer." *PEN Newsletter,* October 1993: 4.

Lopez, Barry, and Frans Lanting. "Lopez-Lanting: A Collaboration." *Audubon* 97, no. 4 (July-August 1995): 68-75.

Margois, Kenneth. "Paying Attention: An Interview with Barry Lopez." *Orion, 9* no. 3, Summer 1990: 50-53.

Martin, Christian. "On Resistance: An Interview with Barry Lopez." *Georgia Review,* Spring 2006, 13-30.

O'Connell, Nicholas. "At One with the Natural World." *Commonweal,* *127,* March 24, 2000: 11-17.

———. "On Sacred Ground: Writer Barry Lopez Respects Alaskan Environment." *Sierra,* November 1998.

PW Forecasts. "Resistance." *Publishers Weekly,* May 3, 2004, 167.

Rueckert, William. "Barry Lopez and the Search for a Dignified and Honorable Relation with Nature." *North Dakota Quarterly, 59,* spring 1991.

Ryan, Laura T. "Higher (Literary) Elevations: Barry Lopez Seeks to Take Readers to New Heights." *Syracuse Herald American,* April 8, 2001, Entertainment sec.

Seaman, Donna. "Barry Lopez." *Booklist,* May 1, 2004, 1547.

Shapiro, Michael. "The Big Rhythm: A Conversation with Barry Lopez on the McKenzie River." *Michigan Quarterly Review* 44, no. 4 (Fall 2005): 583-610.

Shapiro, Michael. "Against the Current: Barry Lopez on Writing about Nature and the Nature of Writing." *The Sun,* no. 366: 4-12.

Sumner, David. "Nature Writing, American Literature, and the Idea of Community-A Conversation with Barry Lopez." *Weber Studies* 18 (Spring 2001): 2-26.

Tydeman, William. "Interview with Barry Lopez." *Northwest Review,* no. 43: February 2006, 96-116.

Warner, Diane. "An Annotated Bibliography of Selected Works by Barry Lopez." *Northwest Review,* no. 43: February 2006, 117-137.

Audiovisual and Sound Recordings

Lopez, Barry. *About This Life: Journeys on the Threshold of Memory.* Read by the author. Los Angeles: Dove Audio. 4 cassettes.

———. "Disturbing the Night." Story as liner notes with *Dark Wood* by David Darling. ECM Records 1519 (1 compact disc).

———. *Light Action in the Caribbean.* Read by the author. HBP 84421 St. Paul, MN: Highbridge. 2 cassettes.

———. *River Notes: The Dance of Herons.* Read by the author. Cello by David Darling. 3534-1. Minocqua, WI: North Word Press. 1 cassette.

———. "Winter Count" (short story) and three essays. Read by the author. AAPL 5021 Columbia, MO: American Audio Prose Library. 1 cassette.

Silverblatt, Michael. *Barry Lopez.* Interview, October 5, 1992, in Los Angeles. VHS. Santa Fe, NM: Lannan Foundation, 1992.

Electronic Sources

Bellwether Prize. "In Support of a Literature of Social Change." http://www.bellwetherprize.org.

Calypso Consulting. "An Interview with Barry Lopez." http://www.calypsoconsulting.com/lopez.html.

Carnegie Centennial Celebration. "Three Rivers Lecture Series." Centennial Lecture Series. http://www.clpgh.org/exhibit/neighborhoods/oakland/oak_centv.html.

Kirkus Reviews. "Resistance." http://web.ebscohost.com.

Lang, Anson. "A Conversation with Barry Lopez." Random House Boldtype. http://www.randomhouse.com/boldtype/1100/lopez/interview.html.

Lopez, Barry. Official Web site. http://www.barrylopez.com.

———. "The Language of Animals." *Resurgence 192.* http://www.resurgenge.org/resurgence/issues/lopez192.htm.

Richards, Linda. "Barry Lopez." http://www.januarymagazine.com/profiles/blopez.html.

Turrentine, Jeff. "Books in Brief: Fiction." *New York Times,* July 4, 2004. http://web.lexis-nexis.com.

Tydeman, William. "Interview with Barry Lopez." *Iron Horse,* Fall, 2003. http://www.english.ttu.edu/IH/Archives/Fall03.htm.

Unpublished Material

Barry Lopez Papers, 1964-2001 and Undated. Southwest Collection/Special Collections Library, Texas Tech University, Lubbock, Texas.

Lopez, Barry. Interview with Barry Lopez. By Mike Newell. October 22 and 23, 1999.

Lopez, Barry, and Mike Newell. Correspondence from May 21, 1999, to March 4, 2008. Private collection.

Index

About Mike Newell

Mike Newell has published three poetry chapbooks—
uNderground Fires, The Unlived Life, and *Aestivation.* His
poems appeared in *Beyond Baroque, Buffalo Spree, Tightrope,
The DeKalb Literary Arts Journal, New Poetry* and *Sulfur* in the
1970s and 1980s. Mike retired from education after twenty-
two roller-coaster years of exchanges of creative energy with
at-risk populations. A wildland firefighter in Alaska in the
1970s and the 1980s, he now works intermittenly on twen-
ty-person hand crews for the United States Forest Service
on Western wildfires. Mike and his lovely wife, Phyllis, share
their log cabin in Upstate New York with their gregarious
lab, Ralph.